WITHDRAWN
0_ / 13 / 2022
SAINT LOUIS UNIVERSITY

SIR WILLIAM EMPSON

GARLAND BIBLIOGRAPHIES OF
MODERN CRITICS AND CRITICAL SCHOOLS
(General Editor: William E. Cain)
Vol. 8

GARLAND REFERENCE LIBRARY
OF THE HUMANITIES
Vol. 376

Garland Bibliographies of Modern Critics and Critical Schools

GENERAL EDITOR:
William E. Cain (Wellesley College)

ADVISORY BOARD:
M.H. Abrams (Cornell University)
Charles Altieri (University of Washington)
Jonathan Culler (Cornell University)
Stanley Fish (Johns Hopkins University)
Gerald Graff (Northwestern University)
Murray Krieger (University of California at Irvine)
Richard Macksey (Johns Hopkins University)
Steven Mailloux (University of Miami)
Edward Said (Columbia University)
Gayatri Chakravorty Spivak (University of Texas at Austin)
René Wellek (Yale University)

SIR WILLIAM EMPSON
An Annotated Bibliography

Frank Day

PR
6009
.M7
Z65
1984

GARLAND PUBLISHING, INC. • NEW YORK & LONDON
1984

© 1984 Frank Day
All rights reserved

Library of Congress Cataloging in Publication Data

Day, Frank, 1932–
Sir William Empson : an annotated bibliography.

(Garland bibliographies of modern critics and critical schools ; vol. 8) (Garland reference library of the humanities ; vol. 376)
Includes index.
1. Empson, William, 1906– —Bibliography.
I. Title. II. Series: Garland bibliographies of modern critics and critical schools ; v. 8. III. Series: Garland reference library of the humanities ; v. 376.
Z8265.6.D38 1984 016.801'95'0924 82-49130
[PR6009.M7]
ISBN 0-8240-9207-4 (alk. paper)

Printed on acid-free, 250-year-life paper
Manufactured in the United States of America

To Elmer, Mona, and Bob

GENERAL EDITOR'S INTRODUCTION

The Garland Bibliographies of Modern Critics and Critical Schools series is intended to provide bibliographic treatment of major critics and critical schools of the twentieth century. Each volume includes an introduction that surveys the critic's life, career, influence, and achievement, or, in the case of the volumes devoted to a critical school, presents an account of its central figures, origins, relation to other critical movements and trends, and the like.

Each volume is fully annotated and contains listings for both primary and secondary materials. The annotations are meant to be ample and detailed, in order to explain clearly, especially for a reader coming to a critic or critical school for the first time, the point and purpose of a book or essay. In this sense, the bibliographies are also designed to be critical guides. We hope that the volumes will inform and stimulate the reader even as they give basic information about what material exists and where it may be located.

We have tried to include as many of the most important critics and critical schools in this series as possible, but some have been omitted. Some critics and critical schools have already received (or are in the process of receiving) adequate treatment, and we see no need to duplicate the efforts of others.

William E. Cain
Wellesley College

CONTENTS

PREFACE

I would not have even begun this "lavish plan," as Sir William has described it, without the careful and reliable bibliography done by Moira Megaw for the *Festschrift* volume edited by Roma Gill. Sir William has told me that even though there may be something missing from the Megaw bibliography, "it can't be of any importance." So my primary debt—a very large one—is to Moira Megaw.

I must also thank Sir William for going over the primary bibliography and informing me of several recent items I had overlooked. These have all been included in this final version.

William Cain, general editor for this series, has been encouraging and helpful. Julia Johnson of Garland Publishing has been more than patient. I am grateful to both of them for their kindness.

I could never have tracked down copies of many of the materials annotated herein without the persistent and inspired work of two members of the inter-library loan staff of the Clemson University library, Marian Withington and Nancy Keffler. I am happy to be able to thank them in print. Carol Marshall of the Chalmers Memorial Library at Kenyon College very obligingly sent me a copy of Empson's piece in the Kenyon *Collegian* about John Crowe Ransom, as well as an essay by George Lanning describing Empson's exploits on the baseball diamond. The latter work was unknown to me, and I am appreciative of her thoughtfulness.

As a general rule, but with a few exceptions, anything I have been able to get my hands on, I have annotated. In a few cases, some customary item in a bibliography entry—such as page numbers—will be found missing. In these instances, I judged the loss in formal completeness to be extenuated by the unusual efforts foreseen as likely.

INTRODUCTION

Cleanth Brooks once called Sir William Empson an "incorrigible amateur,"[1] and I can easily sense what lay behind the remark. It is perhaps what George Fraser had in mind when he said that "People meeting Empson for the first time would say at once, 'This is a poet,' but would be rather surprised to hear, 'This is a Professor of English,' or perhaps even, 'This is a critic.'"[2] Consider the dazzling starts and turns in Empson's career. Among a group of gifted undergraduates at Cambridge in the 1920's, he stood out as one of the best—a student of brilliance and promise in mathematics who switched suddenly to literature and enthusiastically dashed off a book that changed the study of literature drastically in ways that are still being felt. (Muriel Bradbrook has commented on the closeness of his mathematical studies to *Seven Types of Ambiguity*, noting that "His unity of close concentration and wide-ranging perspectives is perhaps the most applied form of applied mathematics that the university of Bertrand Russell has ever turned out."[3]) During these same early years he was writing some of the best of the witty, difficult poems reprinted in most anthologies today. (I. A. Richards discovered lines in them that "resound with an extraordinary and inexplicable passion."[4]) His next book appropriated the pastoral mode for a stunning display of insights developed from Marxist and Freudian views; and this was followed by a foray into linguistic analysis growing out of an involvement in the controversy over the emotive and cognitive theories about language. In the meantime he was reviewing books, taking up the cudgels for Basic English, teaching in Japan, traipsing all over China with the faculty and students of the displaced Chinese universities, and writing a book (unfortunately lost) on the faces of Buddha. He came back to England following World War II and taught at Sheffield University until his retirement in 1971, settling down to battle the Neo-Christians he found entrenched upon his return. He has been, at least, an amateur with authority (as Brooks, always respectful, acknowledges in calling *Complex Words* "provocative and seminal"[5]) and has withstood well the attacks on his scholarship.

Sir William Empson's family belonged to the landed gentry of Yorkshire.[6] By the eighteenth century they had come to live at Yokefleet Hall near the confluence of the Ouse and the Trent, on the site where Empson was born on September 27, 1906. His father was Arthur Reginald Empson, and his mother, Laura, was a Mickelthwait from Barnsley. Empson had an older sister and three older brothers. The oldest, John, was an officer in the Royal Flying Corps and died in a plane crash in 1914. Empson's father died in 1916, and the second son, Arthur, took over the management of the 4,000-acre Yokefleet estate upon his retirement from the army in 1919. Empson went to preparatory school in Folkestone and, in 1920, entered Winchester College as a Scholar. The Gardners have traced his activities there in *The Wykehamist*, the school magazine, sketching his debating activities and pointing out "a nicely ironic touch in his patronizing passing reference to 'country gentlemen' as 'a class no doubt delightful but one which the country could no longer afford to support.'" He also appeared in a production of *Doctor Faustus*, won an English Essay prize, and in 1924 won the Richardson prize in mathematics and a mathematics scholarship to Magdalen College, Cambridge.

Empson went up to Cambridge in October 1925, and the next summer won a First in Part 1 of the Mathematics Tripos. He then switched to studies in English and in 1929 achieved a starred First in Part 1 of the English Tripos. During these years he was a busy reviewer of books and films for *Granta*, the undergraduate journal he served as literary editor, and in June 1927, that periodical printed his first published poem, "Poem about a Ball in the Eighteenth Century." In 1928 he published twenty poems, fifteen of which are included among the fifty-six that make up his *Collected Poems*. He also became co-editor, with Jacob Bronowski and Hugh Sykes Davis, of *Experiment*, a new literary magazine begun at Cambridge in 1928, and his poems made him its pre-eminent contributor.

Empson published *Seven Types of Ambiguity* in 1930, and in

August, 1931, partly thanks to the recommendation of I.A. Richards, his mentor in English at Cambridge, he went by way of the Trans-Siberian Railroad to Japan, where he was to replace Peter Quennell as Professor of English Literature at the Tokyo University of Literature and Science. In 1934 Empson returned to England, and in 1937, after the publication of *Poems* and *Some Versions of Pastoral*, he left once more for the Far East with an appointment as Professor at Peking National University. He travelled through Japanese-occupied Manchuria and arrived in Peking on a Japanese troop train. He then began an adventure unparalleled among other critics, for Peking had fallen to the Japanese and the city's two universities, Pei-ta and Tsinghua, had closed down, as had Nankai University at Tientsin. But the three schools had directed their vacationing students to re-assemble at Changsha, 1,000 miles to the southwest, and Empson had to catch up with them. So he spent the fall term teaching from memory in the mountain village of Nan-yueh, before the schools moved on at the end of 1937 to Kunming on the Burma Road and to Mengtzu, even further southeast.

This is truly a "bizarre and adventurous story," as the Gardners describe it,[7] and one regrets that it has never been told in full. One anecdote from the period was recounted by Empson in "A Chinese University," an essay published in 1940, and it deserves to be retold here not only for its value as history but also for the glimpse it affords of Empson. He had read in Hanoi of some work Eddington had done in physics since Empson had left England, and, being situated in Mengtzu where he was separated from the university scientists in Kunming, he went to Singapore in search of more information from the professors there, only to be "abashed" by their indifference to the Eddington discovery. The rest of the story should be given in his own words:

> But I found myself chatting about it the night I got back to Junming. The train as usual was late; the great Agricultural Institute building where we were accommodated found a blackboard on trestles for me to unpack the bedding on to—in a small room holding two other teachers; I walked off in a hurry to the place where we used to eat, ten minutes' walk, and found only in the moonlight the wreckage where it had been bombed to pieces; so then I came back slowly, asking questions a bit, and altogether I

> missed the dinner; naturally with Chinese methods of eating if you are late there is no dinner left; but luckily somebody had bought food on the train and a tin of salmon had remained in my pocket after I thought I had refused it. So I filled the inevitable Thermos with hot water downstairs (you only drink water hot), and remembered I still had some French brandy, and went back to this cubicle to eat there. By this time the stranger colleagues had turned up and were placidly friendly, accepting the brandy and offering me what they had lying about, dried water-beetles I think it was. Then it turned out one of them was a physicist, so over the salmon and water-beetles I began saying how hard it was to get the truth of this new story about the number of protons in the universe.[8]

The incongruousness of his activity in the midst of national upheaval was not lost on Empson, for later in the same essay he observes that "to puzzle over my lectures on the poet Donne is surely a fantastic war-time occupation." This musing leads to another recollection so typically Empsonian in the telling that it too must be quoted here before leaving the China period in his life:

> A student of economics brought this up in Mengtzu while we were swimming in a rather insanitary little pool used by the villagers for bathing their water-buffalo, and in passing I must tell any millionaire among my readers that no rubber toy for the bath has anything approaching the charm of a water-buffalo. It is curiously slimy, so that to hold on to its tail and try to climb on to its back is one of the major sports.[9]

Empson returned to England in 1940 to work first for the B.B.C.'s Monitoring Department and later its Far Eastern section, where he was a colleague of George Orwell's. In 1941 he married Hester Henrietta Crouse, a South African who also worked for the B.B.C. They have two sons, William Hendrick Mogador and Jacobus Arthur Calais. Empson explains that "each had to have an English name, an Afrikaans name, and the name of a town captured by the Allies on the day he was born."[10]

Empson returned in 1947 to the Peking National University with a subsidy from the British Council, flying to America in 1948 and 1950 to take part in the Kenyon Summer School programs. *The Structure of Complex Words* was published in 1951, rewritten in Peking from material originally written before the war. Empson returned to England in 1952 and became Professor of English Literature at Sheffield University in 1953, remaining there until his retirement in 1971. In the last four decades he has published scarcely any poems, but his criticism has continued steadily, the most notable work, of course, being *Milton's God* in 1961. He now lives in London, and since 1978 he has been Sir William Empson.

Seven Types of Ambiguity

In a review of several books of criticism, including W. K. Wimsatt's *The Verbal Icon* and R. P. Blackmur's *Language and Gesture*, Empson once groused about the concrete universal as a "tiresome paradox" but praised Blackmur as "a great deal more humane and less off the point than these bother-headed theoretical critics."[11] The remark is ironic in light of Empson's own critical practices. Whenever he elaborates an apparatus for exploring a work—the double irony he finds in *Tom Jones*, for instance, or the equations defined in *Complex Words*—one can sense the justice of I.A. Richards's remark about the explanatory chapters that *Complex Words* begins with: Empson's "percipiences . . . are incommensurably more refined than the clumsy terms through which he is . . . trying to control and expound them."[12] Empson seems aware of the difficulties in his comments that "to write good criticism is very hard" and "some kinds of error are best avoided if you just jump at the thing."[13] His first book, *Seven Types of Ambiguity* (1930), is one of the seminal texts of twentieth-century criticism, and it illustrates well Richards's thesis; for in its anatomy of types of ambiguity Empson's scheme is generally judged to have been inadequate,[14] but the ingenuity he displayed in jumping at short texts made him, perhaps, a proto-deconstructionist and, at least, a major influence on the New Criticism. This much is hardly disputed by anyone. It is the evaluation of the book's consequences that has divided critics right from the beginning.

Richards has described the incident that occurred when he was Empson's Director of Studies at Cambridge, and Empson came to him full of enthusiasm for the treatment Laura Riding and Robert Graves had given Shakespeare's sonnet 129 in *A Survey of Modernist Poetry*. After trying his own hand at verbal analysis for a few moments in the meeting, Empson reportedly remarked, "You could do that with any poetry, couldn't you?" Richards then sent him on his way to work at the new game, and in two weeks Empson had the "central 30,000 words" of *Seven Types*.[15]

The gestation of *Seven Types*—the story of the famous tutor and his brilliant pupil—is a matter of great interest, and James Jensen has tried to explain why the book fails "to rationalize and implement a coherent critical theory." He speculates that the "genius of the book is at odds with its structure" simply because Empson jumped at the thing in the beginning, only to have Richards insist that an "objective structure" be given the analyses as the only way to save the work from appearing "an unredeemed act of egoism." Eventually, Jensen thinks, they worked out the apparatus of the typology in conference and Empson wrote the manuscript by himself.[16] Richards's comment on Jensen's hypothesis was, "This seems to me not *bad* fiction and I've no wish to offer any rival account."[17] Empson's response was to deny any instruction from Richards in writing *Seven Types*.[18]

In his preliminary remarks on "ambiguity," Empson warns that he will use the word in an "extended sense," seeking "alternative reactions to the same piece of language." He admits that "Sometimes . . . the word may be stretched absurdly far, but it is descriptive because it suggests the analytical approach, and with that I am concerned." He realizes that the seven types are to a great extent "merely a convenient framework," and he anticipates one common criticism when he explains that his value judgments are implicit in his choices of works to discuss: "I shall almost always take poems that I admire."[19] He thus seems to have been alert to the objections critics would make to his approach and been concerned to neutralize them at the beginning.

He was not wholly successful, however. *Seven Types* is probably still "the major, and continuing, stimulus to descriptive criticism in England,"[20] but there are several interrelated points on which it has been attacked repeatedly. For instance, despite Empson's explanation that he treats only works that he admires, he has been indicted for failing to make value judgments. Muriel Bradbrook, writing in *Scrutiny* in 1933, insists that intelligence and sensitivity are not sufficient by themselves in criticism and that *Seven Types* lacks "judgment, a sense of relative values without which criticism is no more than a game for the intelligent and an emotional shower bath."[21] R.G. Cox repeats this criticism in *Scrutiny* fifteen years later and decries Empson for having contributed to "a relaxation of discipline" and "various kinds of irresponsible eccentricity."[22] Geoffrey Strickland's condemnation goes even further, for he claims that "It is impossible to conceive the organic growth of the sensibility without its continuity of judgment."[23]

Dissatisfaction with Empson's "fierce and minute scrutiny of short texts," as Tillyard describes the method of *Seven Types*,[24] is common among those critics who feel criticism must cope with the whole text of a work. There are in addition, those social critics—like the *Scrutiny* reviewers—who identify a corpus of works that embody the values and traditions of a culture, and Marxist critics who stress the relations between poetry, ideology, and history. Edwin Berry Burgum, for example, complains that the method of *Seven Types* "ignores the social or historical referent."[25] Burgum's Marxist attitudes are complemented by the contempt Alfred Kazin expresses for Empson's work. Kazin sneers at "lay scientists of letters" and "field scientists of metaphor" who offer "a substitute for the loose chitchat of nonscientific minds." Instead of finding that Empson has given criticism credibility by his rational approach, Kazin accuses him of having "raised the professional prestige of criticism at the expense of every human need of literature as prophecy or history or sustenance."[26] For these critics, texts are documents of writ and human life which we murder when we dissect them.

There are also those aesthetic critics, like John Crowe Ransom, who insist that the organic unity of a work should be mirrored in the completeness of the analysis devoted to it. Thus Ransom admires the "extreme intelligence" of Empson's commentary but deplores the lack in his criticism of a proper attention to structure. He finds it "extremely important to recognize and approve such logical structure as a poem may have; its texture of meanings should find a structure to attach itself to. The poets are not quite irresponsible, and the readers should not be more irresponsible than the poets."[27]

It is illuminating that this remark comes in Ransom's epochal work, *The New Criticism*, for Empsonian analysis is standard practice for the New Critics, and Ransom is here defining its place among the critic's competencies. He realizes the full importance of the technique, noting that "Richards and Empson have spread quickly" and that it is therefore "time to identify a powerful intellectual movement that deserves to be called a new criticism."[28]

Burgum echoes Ransom's remark ten years later, saying that *Seven Types* "almost begins a new era in the criticism of poetry," and he also cavils at Empson's predisposition to favor "the poetry of the casuist." For Burgum, Empson's method in *Seven Types* "sets up a tendency to regard the value of the poem as proportional to the quantity of ambiguity in it."[29] Demurring over the analyses has been a common response. Even though Cleanth Brooks thinks that *Seven Types* "reads for the most part like uncommonly good talk" and praises it for making metaphor and metrics functional,[30] many others have been critical. F.R. Leavis, for instance, judges *Seven Types* "that rare thing, a critical work of the first order" but nevertheless feels that Empson is "apt to be a little too ingenious in detecting ambiguities."[31] Leavis's judgment is mild compared to that of F. W. Bateson in his denunciation of Empson's analysis of Shakespeare's "bare, ruined choirs," a passage which becomes for him a "characteristic specimen of Empsonian irresponsibility."[32] René Wellek objects to "a method of verbal analysis which often loses all contact with the text and indulges in private associations."[33] And finally, Charles Glicksberg speaks for many, certainly, in his solemn caution that "for those who are interested primarily in poetry and only secondarily in the virtuosity of the critic, Empson's work and that of his followers must be rejected as misleading, sometimes dangerously so."[34]

These are some of the reservations of powerful critics, and they surely point to controversies that have become pronounced in critical theory recently. Empson's criticism raises, for instance, questions about the fixed identity of the text as opposed to the reader's freedom of play. Is the critic himself creative, elevating works to greatness by creative readings of them? Even though he proclaims repeatedly his attention to the objective meaning of the author, Empson's ingenious scrutiny of texts leads ironically to the many reprimands for his "irresponsibility." But others have reacted differently. Mario Praz shows great originality in comparing Empson to Salvador Dali. "The same type of attention spellbound by magnificent minutiae which we find in Salvadore Dali's paintings is witnessed in Empson's exploration . . . of all possible meanings of words and the consequent opening of strange perspectives in the pages of classics: these, then, acquire a 'tension,' a dramatic irony which is not unlike certain effects of surrealism."[35] One would like for Praz to have said more on this subject. Michael Wood is another who praises those very elements in *Seven Types* that others have criticized. He stresses the ludic element in the analyses, praising *Seven Types* as a "mischievous book . . . which delights in multiplying complicated meanings" to give more "sheer pleasure" than any other of Empson's works.[36]

The intensity of many of these responses suggests that most critics would agree with Graham Hough that Empson began the search for "multiple and simultaneous meaning" in poetry.[37] Hough calls *Seven Types* "a commando raid on . . . what conventional criticism has been content to regard as ineffable" and he thinks that Empson's approach has been "quietly absorbed into the canon of modern literary criticism."[38] And for those who think a text is more than "a piece of language," to use a phrase of Empson's, Hough's appraisal of the influence of *Seven Types* points to a great philosophical crisis in modern literary theory.

Ransom spoke of a new criticism, and E.M.W. Tillyard carries the analysis further in his account of the "revolution in English studies at Cambridge between 1918 and 1935." He refers to the importance of *Seven Types* in forming the principles of the revolution, and his judgment is acrid and memorable: "Anyone quick to distinguish the rotten from the ripe and to sniff the taint of incipient corruption might now have guessed that an impulse had attained its maximum strength and that henceforward a decline or a coarsening might be expected."[39] Thus Wood's "mischievous" and playful *Seven Types* is seen differently by those who share Tillyard's sensibility.

E.D. Hirsch is one of those who condemn *Seven Types* as heretical, concluding that it "demonstrates on almost every page what happens to interpretation when a text is self-consciously perceived to be "'a piece of language,' and the problem of validity is ignored."[40] Behind this pattern of error and irresponsibility (or satisfying play, if you like) is a vision of the world that is radically flawed, Empson's keenest critics feel. Hirsch has defined the issues for literary criticism, but Hugh Kenner, over the years, has been the most powerful critic of everything Empson has done, and in his review of Empson's *Collected Poems* he has stated definitively the case against Empson: "The poetry and the criticism alike are the products of a single, disciplined, but 'period,' sensibility for which anything may mean anything because nothing has ontological meaning; and endless logical constructions are the sum of all human activity."[41] One might quarrel with "period" perhaps, but probably how one feels about the vision condemned here will be crucial in how one feels about Empson.

Empson has answered the two main charges against him—that the analyses in *Seven Types* are inadequate because they do not serve a judgment-making impulse and that the analyses stray irresponsibly far from their texts and thus betray a "sensibility for which anything may mean anything." In "My Credo: Verbal Analysis," published in 1950, Empson defends the kind of criticism that tries to show "how the machine is meant to work, and therefore to show all its working parts in order."[42] Moreover, he explains that complexity is not a gauge of value in his criticism. Rather, one begins with an intuitive sense of the merit of a work, proceeding to examine the "profound complexities" assumed to be there. But a passage is not necessarily bad if it lacks complexity, and the critic need not have to revise his initial judgment if complexities do not emerge in the analysis. Empson affirms the place of valuation in criticism but says of his own work that "to assess the value of the poem as a whole is not the primary purpose of this kind of criticism."[43] The statement seems mild enough, but it is not likely to have converted many of his critics. Disputants who cannot accept this credo will probably find no more dialogue possible.

Empson has defended himself against the charge of irresponsibility in his frequent statements of the need to know the author's mind. As early as 1928 he remarks that "The Robert Graves' school of criticism is only impressive when the analysis it employs becomes so elaborate as to score a rhetorical triumph; when each word in the line is given four or five meanings, four or five reasons for sounding right and suggesting the right things."[44] By "the right things" is presumably meant some objective meaning put there by the author. He refuses to abandon the authority of the author's mind. Even though he says once that Dylan Thomas "half the time is not 'saying anything' in the ordinary meaning of the term,"[45] a few years later he disputes Cyril Connolly's claim that Thomas's power defies analysis, insisting that "there is something there which I feel and can't see, but could see."[46] Like the relations between sound and sense, which he claims in *Seven Types* are capable of being understood "if we knew a great deal,"[47] some meanings remain unclear only because of our limited knowledge. Thus Empson refuses to surrender to the Intentional Fallacy, arguing that it would mean "the students are denied any spontaneous contact with an author's mind."[48] He similarly rejects—with contempt—the dogma that the reader must not know anything outside the text, maintaining that any strategy is valid that leads to a firmer grasp on authorial intention.[49]

Determination to know the author's mind takes Empson to dangerous limits in his interpretation of "The Ancient Mariner." Speaking of one passage in that poem, Empson says that "we are printing what Coleridge is not known to have written, but what he at least would have written if he had decided to keep the verse which he had long before designed for this place."[50] And those critics who do not stress an intention, an idea, in a work are found wanting, as when Empson complains of Cleanth Brooks that "Truth" is something "which Mr. Brooks wants to keep out of poetry" and says of Brooks's "cast-iron program" that it doesn't go "all the way."[51] His review of Wallace Stevens's *Selected Poems* reveals the same prejudice for a strong content of ideas. He admires the "new fancy dress" in Steven's language but grouses that "One can't help wishing he had found more to say, if only because he could evidently say it."[52] If he were truly a critic devoted to spinning solipsistic fancies from others' works, one would think that Thomas and Stevens would be especially suggestive for his purposes.

Some Versions of Pastoral

The seven essays in *Some Versions of Pastoral* present somewhat different considerations. First, they deal more with whole works and therefore offer a much broader kind of analysis. Second, they take up topics of class and society in a way that prompts Stanley Hyman to call *Some Versions* "implicitly Marxist throughout."[53] Third, they frequently reveal the influence of ideas from cultural anthropology, and the much-acclaimed essay on *Alice in Wonderland* demonstrates what Empson could do with insights gained from Freud. The essays are rich with fresh observations but sometimes the overall pattern of their argument is difficult to follow, as Arthur Mizener notes when he complains that Empson explains too little.[54] Paul Alpers agrees that *Some Versions* is difficult to use but explains unconvincingly that the oblique style is Empson's way of "dealing with the central puzzle of freedom and determinism."[55]

The reader is sympathetic and ready to be convinced, but often feels that too much knowledge on his part may have been assumed by the writer. Most frustrating is the lack of some kind of direct statement of the notion of pastoral that binds these essays together. Roger Sale struggles to trace a unifying thematic progression through the separate pieces, but he seems to try too hard and eventually loses the reader's confidence.[56] A familiar criticism, brought up by Ransom in his discussion of the Marvell essay, is the old charge of self-indulgence. Ransom laments "Mr. Empson's almost inveterate habit of over-reading poetry" and admits that he is "afraid of the rise of a doctrine which would teach that the poem is what we make it."[57]

Despite these reservations and despite the challenge of sorting out what Kenneth Burke calls "a welter of observations that suffer from lack of selectivity and drive,"[58] *Some Versions* does, however, provide an understanding of the pastoral that has two foci: first, the process of "putting the complex into the simple,"[59] and second, pastoral's role as a "unifying social force" that offers a "means of bridging differences and reconciling social classes"[60]. A great deal of Empson's version of pastoral appears to have much in common with Wordsworth's exaltation of "humble and rustic life" in the preface to the second edition of *Lyrical Ballads*. Specifically, "putting the complex into the simple" is a restatement of Wordsworth's explanation that "Humble and rustic life was generally chosen . . . because in that condition of life our elementary feelings coexist in a state of greater simplicity, and, consequently, may be more accurately contemplated, and more forcibly communicated." The Wordsworth passage has an even closer parallel in the essay on Marvell's "The Garden," where Empson says that one of his assumptions is "that you can say everything about complex people by a complete consideration of simple people."[61] Furthermore, in the essay on *The Beggar's Opera*, Empson says that pastoral "describes the lives of simple 'low' people to an audience of refined wealthy people, so as to make them think first, 'this is true about everyone' and then 'this is specifically true about us.'"[62] Thus, pastoral becomes, in Alpers' phrase, a "unifying social force." Empson sums this all up in his assertion that both heroic and pastoral "assume or preach . . . a proper or beautiful relation between rich and poor."[63]

This is all well said, but how it makes *Some Versions* "implicitly Marxist throughout," as Hyman has described it and no one has risen up to deny, is not completely clear. A genre that preaches "a proper or beautiful relation between rich and poor" might sound more like counter-revolutionary pap to some—and even sentimental to others. There is, however, a sort of Marxist ganging-up on the Philistines, the vulgar middle class of profits and poor taste, lurking in the admiration of "refined wealthy people" for "'simple' low people" and especially in the "identification of the refined, the universal, and the low" that Empson calls "the whole point of pastoral."[64] Empson has pre-empted my criticism, though, in speaking of the aristocrat's "obvious function for the people" in the Border ballads and of the way "they are pleased to describe his grandeur and fine clothes."[65] His view of class relations is idyllic: "they were class-conscious all right, but not conscious of class war. Pastoral is a queerer business, but I think permanent and not dependent on a system of class exploitation."[66] Who, however, today would take this remark seriously: "Any socialist state with an intelligentsia at the capital that felt itself more cultivated than the farmers . . . could produce it; it is common in present-day Russian films, and a great part of their beauty. . . ."[67]

If for the other six essays the implicit Marxism reduces to this vision of the beautiful relation between refined people and simple, low people, the essay on "Proletarian Literature" does address numerous complicated issues of class and politics. The commentary on Gray's "Elegy"[68] perhaps seems at first reading strongly Marxist because Empson accuses Gray of making it appear "that we ought to accept the injustice of society as we do the inevitability of death." But that is not Empson's final remark. It simply leads to a more fundamental affirmation that "what is said is one of the permanent truths; it is only in degree that any improvement of society could prevent wastage of human powers; the waste even in a fortunate life, the isolation even of a life rich in intimacy, cannot but be felt deeply, and is the central feeling of tragedy." This is one of the most moving statements in Empson's criticism and seriously undercuts any satisfaction a Marxist would take in the analysis. Even so, Empson admits that the "great poetic statements" of Gray's truth are "bourgeois" and "suggest to many readers, though they do not say, that for the poor man things cannot be improved even in degree." His last word on this subject, however, is that "one could not estimate the amount of bourgeois ideology 'really in' the verse from Gray."[69] It would be difficult, I would judge, to call this a rich Marxist reading of Gray.

Indeed, the whole intent of "Proletarian Literature" is to distinguish that genre from pastoral, demonstrating the latter's superiority ("I think good proletarian art is usually Covert Pastoral"[70]) and its rarity in England. Empson admits he did find the pastoral in "watching Spaniards tread out sherry grapes and squeeze the skins afterwards," and the remark reveals a lot about his understanding of pastoral. Even though these Spaniards were not living "simple pretty lives," "some quality in their own very harsh lives made them feel at home with the rest of civilisation, not suspicious of it."[71] But there can never be pure proletarian art, Empson says, because "the artist must be one with the worker,"[72] which is impossible "because the artist never is quite at one with any public." In fact, he concludes, proletarian literature is "a bogus concept."[73]

Despite his suspicion of the bourgeois class, Empson is hardly ready to submit to the standard line on alienation: "When communists say that an author under modern capitalism feels cut off from most of the life of the country, and would not under communism, the remark has a great deal of truth, though he might only exchange a sense of isolation for a sense of the waste of his powers; it is certainly not so completely true as to make the verse from Gray pointless to a man living under communism."[74] At this point in his argument he explains that the conventions of pastoral have worked for social unity and against a crippling sense of isolation. Given these conclusions, it might be more accurate to say that *Some Versions of Pastoral* engages Marxism in a thoughtful dialogue rather than that it is "implicitly Marxist throughout." Empson tells in 1963 of his Socialist sympathies for the "pylon poets" in the 1930's ("I'm very sorry I wasn't in on it")[75], but he hardly kept a strict party line in his criticism in those days.

The Structure of Complex Words

The Structure of Complex Words combines the central interests of the two earlier books. Empson spells this out clearly:

> Of the prose books, *Ambiguity* examines the complexity of meaning in poetry; *Pastoral* examines the way a form for reflecting a social background without obvious reference to it is used in a historical series of literary works, and *Complex Words* is on both those topics; it offers a general theory about the interaction of a word's meaning and takes examples which cover rather the same historical ground as *Pastoral*. Roughly, the moral is that a developing society decides practical questions more by the way it interprets words it thinks obvious and traditional than by its official statements of current dogma.[76]

What this statement doesn't indicate is the extent to which *Complex Words* is a repudiation of emotive theories of language and, thus, a distancing of Empson from Richards (to whom the book is dedicated). It is not that Empson denies that words carry a freight of feelings, only that he discovers in Richards's books "a series of phrases to the effect that the Emotions given by words in poetry are independent of their Sense"—a doctrine that he feels, "if taken at all simply, would be sure to lead to bad criticism."[77] And Empson, who advocates "argufying" in verse and thinks that in Dylan Thomas's poetry "there is something there which I feel and can't see, but could see," rejects Richards's position that "the function of poetry is to call out an Attitude which is not dependent on any belief open to disproof by facts."[78] When he completes his analysis, it turns out that the role of emotion in a word is "merely as a term for what was left behind when various other elements . . . had been separated out."[79] Thus, emotion is a kind of slag remaining after the meaning has been refined.

Empson elaborates in his dense second chapter, "Statements in Words," an apparatus for breaking down words into their subatomic components. The basic idea is suggested in a brief review written in 1930: ". . . our stress on the complexity of words has increased, so that a single word has come to be thought of as a complex molecule which must not be unpacked in ordinary use."[80] What his "bits of machinery" attempt to do is systematize this unpacking.

The response to this undertaking has followed the pattern of much of the criticism of Empson's work: more or less indifference to the theory but warm appreciation of the practical results. Brooks, for instance, calls the analysis of *wit* in Pope's *Essay on Criticism* "brilliant and convincing" but sees no difference between the linguistic analysis practiced here and that used in *Seven Types*.[81] Michael Wood finds Empson's system unexciting and says that Empson "can seem downright cautious and plodding in comparison with his flighty French contemporaries."[82] One reviewer describes Empson's semantic equations as "perplexing at first" and thinks that "they perhaps need a special type of mind to handle them adequately." But the same reviewer judges *Complex Words* as "unquestionably the most important contribution to critical theory since *The Sacred Wood*."[83] So Graham Hough is representative of the critical consensus in his verdict that the analytical machinery is "ill-chosen and unmemorable" but the essays are "brilliant and deeply thought."[84]

Only Hugh Kenner dissents. He thinks the critical apparatus is logical enough but useless to the critic. The book is "disappointing," Kenner concludes, a collection of "disjunct" essays employing a method that is unsuited for opening up long poems and ineffective with concrete images.[85] Kenner detects behind Empson's approach to criticism an assumption that words are subjective, an assumption that reduces Empson's endeavors to mere exercises in personal satisfaction. His summing up is unsparing: "he has accommodated himself to his own image of the Victorian scientist, who was 'believed to have discovered a new kind of Roman virtue,' and whom the public could always surprise, as Alice did the White Knight, obliviously head down in his suit of armor, hung with bellows and beehives, 'patiently labouring at his absurd but fruitful conceptions.'"[86]

Kenner's charge that words are subjective for Empson suggests a relativism in Empson's thought that he has tried to avoid by appealing to a common sense belief in the shared understanding and experience of other people. This belief is most explicitly stated in the three appendices to *Complex Words*, where he makes some of his most direct statements of his convictions on philosophical issues. Regardless of what may be inferred from his practice in poetry and criticism, his discussion in Appendix I, "Theories of Value," holds out a claim for a special objective basis for value and meaning; for he says, in answer to C. L. Stevenson in *Ethics and Language*, "I think something can be said to make more definite the idea of a correspondence between a moral feeling and the universe or the outer world."[87] Although he sees no religious basis for objective standards of value and meaning (and reports "that the idea of God cannot healthily be used as a fiction on the mere ground that it does you good"),[88] he erects a system of value on the conviction that "whatever is a good state of being is good in other people as well as me, so it is good to see that they get it."[89] He admits there is a regress built into the notion that it is good to be good, and also that "These flat little fundamental problems are wonderfully slippery," but he concludes that "it seems clear that the fundamental step here is not an emotive one."[90] Readers like Kenner will find these arguments painful and distorted, but for Empson the bedrock of systems of value is human rationality: "It is a part of the process of believing that there is a real world outside you, an idea which is built up by generalisation and analogy. . . ."[91]

"Theories of Value" is a brilliant essay, broad in understanding and eloquent in expression. It is one of the best things Empson has written and deserves to be more widely discussed, especially by those interested in Stanley Fish's notion of interpretive communities. Unless one insists that a value system has to be externally grounded—as I suppose Kenner does—and faults Empson's reasoning by some kind of analogy to Gödel's Proof, then Empson's rational appeal to community should be esteemed for its avoidance of egoism. If it's ultimately judged to be a sleight-of-hand trick in logic, then it's at least as convincing a magic show as any other under the big tent.

Milton's God and the Neo-Christians

Empson asserts brusquely in *Seven Types*[92] a doctrine that explains what a critic should do as he writes with complete confidence in the shared experience of his readers:

> It is the business of the critic to extract for his public what it wants; to organise, what he may indeed create, the taste of his period. So that literature in so far as it is a living matter, demands a sense, not so much of what is really there, as of what is necessary to carry a particular situation "off."[93]

What Empson has done with the "living matter" of English literature has been to try to de-Christianize and de-Symbolize many of the classic works, purging them of non-rational elements and presenting them as narratives continuous with human experience and reflecting a world that does not trick the common-sense realist.

His approach is dramatized most vividly, of course, in *Milton's God*. The central idea of that work is stated in 1953, eight years before the book appeared: the "startling irreducible confusions" in *Paradise Lost* "so far from proving that the poem is bad, explain *why* it is so good."[94] The impulse behind the book derives great power from Empson's hatred of the Christian God, whom he describes as "the wickedest thing yet invented by the black heart of man."[95] The book's argument was generally poorly received, but even among his supporters there is a sense that *Milton's God* is a "work of obsession."[96] Denis Donoghue, for instance, thinks that his hatred of Christianity is the "most tedious part"[97] of Empson's mind, and George Fraser protests that "Milton is a bad stick to beat Christianity with," even though he admits the book has "splendid vigour."[98] Probably W. W. Robson has been the most perceptive and dispassionate of the critics of *Milton's God*. Robson admits the book is a welcome corrective to the "eccentric" views of Tillyard and C. S. Lewis, and he applauds Empson's attack on "critics for whom 'humanist' and 'liberals' are words of abuse."[99] He concludes, however, that as an attack on Christianity *Milton's God* is "confused and inconsequent" and "does not remove the incoherences in *Paradise Lost*, but increases one's sense of them."[100]

A great deal of the interpretation concerns issues that resist resolution to everyone's satisfaction, such as the excellently argued claim that Milton expected God to abdicate by giving up his transcendental, anthropomorphic being and "dissolve into the landscape and become immanent only."[101] But at the same time Empson achieves some powerful triumphs. The following point seems to me unanswerable except by frantic polemic: "a parent who 'foresaw' that the children would fall and then insisted upon exposing them to the temptation in view would be considered neurotic, if nothing worse; and this is what we must ascribe to Milton's God."[102] One may protest that it is unfair to read *Paradise Lost* as a narrative continuous with human experience and to judge the characters accordingly. But it is an easily defended and standard practice of Empson's. This is the Empson who is a throwback to the Enlightenment and the Empson whom John Heath-Stubbs has in mind when he admits that Empson's attack on Christianity "takes its rise from a fundamental human decency and detestation of cruelty and intolerance."[103] Heath-Stubb's defence of the Christian God, however, is especially impressive because it is naturalistic: "It seems at least as likely that the corruption of power, and the perennial desire of the human herd to enforce conformity to itself were as responsible for these enormities as any metaphysical conception."[104]

The Major Essays

Paul Alpers provides the key to understanding the sensibility behind the fluent, disputatious essays on Ben Jonson, Donne, Fielding, Shakespeare, Dryden, Coleridge, Yeats, and Joyce. Alpers notes Empson's aversion to tragic and metaphysical visions and explains: "The human condition, to him, is always historical and social, and on the highest throne in the world we are still sitting only on our own rump."[105] This is very surely true. Empson condemns, for instance, the "pietistic writing"[106] in Robert Heilman's study of *King Lear*, charging Heilman with being "blindly inhumane"[107] in saying that Cordelia and Gloucester deserve their fates: "in Mr. Heilman's case there is a necessity to distribute blame in this absurd way, because he is determined to justify Nature and the gods."[108] Similarly, Empson alleges political bias in Dover Wilson's "preaching to us about his Medieval Vice and Ideal King,"[109] accusing Dover Wilson of a need to explain away the "pathetic description" of Falstaff's death and thereby justify the "modern royalist"[110] in his respect for Hal. Maynard Mack is reproved for "imposing an essentially medieval 'vision'" on *Lear*, eschewing any effort to "elucidate motives or excite human interest,"[111] a point of view repeated in Empson's introduction to *Narrative Poems by Shakespeare* in the emphasis he puts on the "human or experiential reality of the poems."[112]

The two splendid essays on *Volpone* and *The Alchemist* are all of a piece with the writings on Shakespeare's plays. Empson says "the pietistic strain in Eng. Lit." has produced "crippled or perverted moral judgments, wholly out of contact with the basic folly of the older works which they purport to interpret."[113] *Volpone* demands indulgence in a hearty "rogue sentiment," and you should be prepared to "fare jovially, and clap your hands"[114] at the end. As for *The Alchemist*, it is not so, Empson says, that Jonson "hates and despises"[115] all his characters, and furthermore, Empson adds, we need not be "so solemn as is now usual over the repeated claims of Jonson to be an improving author."[116] Finally, Jonson did not loathe luxury or feel "hatred and contempt for science."[117]

Empson has attempted in a series of passionately argued essays to "rescue" John Donne.[118] Fundamental to his position is a sympathy with the twenties' view that "Donne in his earlier poetry held broad and enlightened views on church and state, that he was influenced by the great scientific discoveries, and that he used the theme of freedom in love partly as a vehicle for these ideas to show what the ideological and sociological effects of Paracelsus and Copernicus would turn out to be."[119] A fruitful result of Donne's interest in science, Empson says, was his speculation about life on other planets and the attendant theological implications, and, most importantly, prominent use of the theme of the separate planet in numerous poems. Thus, Empson objects to Rosemond Tuve's argument for the centrality of the rhetorical tradition in Donne's poetry, complaining that analysis of Donne's rhetoric "tends to 'explain things away.'"[120] A related point in all of his discussions is the superiority of Grierson's text of Donne's poems to that established by Helen Gardner.[121]

Of twentieth-century writers, Empson has discussed Yeats and Joyce with the most fervor. He struggles to deflect symbolist readings of Yeats, fussing that "it is a basic trouble about critics who revere 'symbolism' that they will not allow the literal meaning any weight at all."[122] He says of "Sailing to Byzantium" that "the poem feels much better if one takes a waking interest in the story; there is no need to say that its merit resides in the confusion at a deep level which seems to be inherent in symbolist technique."[123]

Empson identifies Joyce as the only great writer in English in the first half of this century not to be aligned politically with the Fascists.[124] He responds fiercely to what he calls the "Kenner Smear,"[125] denying Kenner's claim that Stephen Dedalus is not meant to be the young Joyce but only some errant youth who, Empson says, "can never grow into the wise old author (intensely Christian, though in a mystically paradoxical way) who writes the book."[126] No less wrong, he thinks, is the view that Joyce relented in his bitterness toward the Church, this being, in Empson's mind, a canard fostered by the Neo-Christian "majority of Eng. Lit. critics, especially in America."[127] To one critic's attempt to show that Joyce made his peace with the Church, Empson replies harshly: "He also would think it a betrayal to twist his writings into propaganda for the worship of the torture-monster."[128] In their humanism and respect for narrative, his interpretations of Yeats and Joyce are consistent with his readings of the older writers.

George Fraser's sketch of the "moral framework" of Empson's poems is equally valid in describing his criticism. Fraser finds in the poems

> a religious temperament, a scientific world view, the attitude toward politics of a traditional English liberal of the best kind, a constitutional melancholy and a robust good-humour, a sardonic wit, a gift for expressing the diffidence and passion of romantic personal attachments, a belief in pleasure, a scepticism about abstract systems, and a sharply practical impatience with anything he considers cant.[129]

It is unnecessary to elaborate at length on Fraser's anatomy of the Empsonian sensibility, but a few remarks will be useful by way of conclusion.

For instance, the "religious temperament" that Fraser mentions is revealed clearly in Empson's "Final Reflections" on *Milton's God* included in the 1981 reprint of that work. He clarifies his own feelings about God with the explanation that "What is known of the universe so far is astoundingly wonderful and beautiful, and I am glad that I was born."[130] It seems exactly the confession of faith to expect from Empson.

As for his being a "traditional English liberal of the best kind," he affirms his Benthamite convictions several times in his criticism. He spurns the politics of Wyndham Lewis, Yeats, Eliot, Pound, and Lawrence in one essay, identifying them with what he calls "the basic Christian tradition as enshrined in the textbooks of Unnaturalism, *Les Fleurs du Mal, A Rebours,* and *The Portrait of Dorian Gray*"[131]—not perhaps every reader's sense of the Christian tradition. He then defends Benthamism and praises Joyce for avoiding the "political and religious fashions" paraded by these reactionaries.[132] He repeats the statement of his Benthamite beliefs in his essay for the Richards *Festschrift,* where he praises Richards for beliefs that inform the whole body of Empson's criticism.[133]

I want to point last to Fraser's discernment of both "a constitutional melancholy and a robust good-humour" in the poems.

Perhaps these elements are not so nicely balanced in the criticism as in the poetry, but they do seem to me united there in a significant way. The harmonious co-existence of Empson's melancholy and his good-humor reveals his own kind of negative capability. A. E. Rodway acknowledges this strength in Empson and praises him for being "perhaps the only modern poet to have refused to retreat from, flinch at, posture before, or simply defy, the fact that 'Life involves maintaining oneself between contradictions'"[134] (as Empson says in *Seven Types*). Rodway concludes that this is Empson's "chief general theme" and notes that it is "frequently and significantly . . . embodied in fire images"[135] in the poems. His observation strikes me as true. Christopher Ricks, as well, stresses the importance to Empson of the tension of life's contradictions, but he may go too far in concluding "that the complex of thinking and feeling involved in begetting—man's desire to raise posterity—is 'the right handle to take hold of the bundle,' or at any rate a right handle, in considering Empson's poems."[136] I prefer another handle, an image from a poem much discussed by Empson, the twelfth line of Shakespeare's Sonnet 73: "Consum'd with that which it was nourish'd by." This line, with its logical paradox and its fire image, seems to me to embody most satisfactorily the spirit animating Empson's work. That we are eventually consumed by the passions that nourish us is one of life's melancholy contradictions that Empson has stood up to with good humour.

But I am talking only about handles, and this kind of speculation can get out of control. It is only necessary to say that the poet and the critic seem of imagination all one compact and that the achievement seems considerable. And there seems an excellent chance that Karl Miller will prove to be far-sighted in judging that "it can, after all, be assumed that his teachings will have a long run, that they will be mediated, and made doctrinal, to a nation that has not yet come into being."[137]

NOTES

1. "Hits and Misses," p. 677. (Below, J22.)

2. "The Man within the Name: William Empson as Poet, Critic, and Friend," p. 53. (Below, I32.)
3. "The Ambiguity of William Empson," p. 260. (Below, J17a.)
4. "The Poetry of William Empson," p. 260. (Below, J17a.)
5. "Hits and Misses," p. 678.
6. All of the biographical information in the following sketch is taken from the introduction to *The God Approached* by Philip and Averill Gardner. (Below, H2.)
7. *The God Approached*, p. 26.
8. "A Chinese University," p. 240. (Below, D28.)
9. "A Chinese University," p. 244.
10. *Twentieth-Century Authors, First Supplement. A Biographical Dictionary of Modern Literature*, p. 307. (Below, D50.)
11. "Still the Strange Necessity," p. 479. (Below, D51.)
12. "Semantic Frontiersman," p. 102. (Below, I83.)
13. Review of D. G. James, *Scepticism and Poetry*; David Daiches, *New Literary Values*; Dallas Kenmare, *The Future of Poetry*; Martin Gilkes, *Introduction to Modern Poetry*; Bhawani Shankar, *Modern English Poetry*, p. 705. (Below, F44.)
14. The entry under "Ambiguity" in the *Longman Companion to Twentieth Century Literature* (1981) is representative: "The celebrated seven types proved in the long run a set of distinctions without differences and the book remained principally valuable for its close readings of a series of poetic extracts. As a demonstration of a hierarchy of complexity it was deemed to have failed." Cleanth Brooks makes the same point when he states that the framework of *Seven Types* is defective but defends the "brilliant asides" and "analytical commentaries" as "the important thing." (I10, p. 503.)
15. "William Empson," Supplement. (Below, M44.)
16. "The Construction of *Seven Types of Ambiguity*," p. 243, (Below, I54.)
17. Letter, p. 255. (Below, L27.)
18. Letter, pp. 257–8. (Below, G71.)
19. *Seven Types of Ambiguity*, pp. 1–7. (Below, A1b.)

20. Roger Fowler and Peter Mercer, "Criticism and the Language of Literature," p. 55. (Below, I31.)
21. "The Criticism of William Empson," p. 257. (Below, J2.)
22. "Ambiguity Revised," p. 151. (Below, J3.)
23. "The Criticism of William Empson," p. 331. (Below, I94.)
24. E.M.W. Tillyard, *The Muse Unchained: An Intimate Account of the Revolution in English Studies at Cambridge*, p. 130. (Below, M59.)
25. "The Cult of the Complex in Poetry," p. 32. (Below, I13.)
26. *On Native Grounds*, p. 445. (Below, M22.)
27. *The New Criticism*, p. 125. (Below, I81.)
28. *The New Criticism*, p. 130.
29. "The Cult of the Complex in Poetry," p. 32.
30. "Empson's Criticism," p. 497. (Below, I10.)
31. "Empson's Criticism," p. 257. (Below, J4a.)
32. "The Function of Criticism at the Present Time," p. 8. (Below, I4.)
33. "The Main Trends of Twentieth-Century Criticism," p. 104. (Below, I106.)
34. "William Empson: Genius of Ambiguity," p. 377. (Below, I40.)
35. "Historical and Evaluative Criticism," p. 70. (Below, I77.)
36. "Incomparable Empson," p. 31. (Below, K9.)
37. "An Eighth Type of Ambiguity," p. 76. (Below, I51.)
38. *Style and Stylistics*, p. 91. (Below, I52.)
39. *The Muse Unchained: An Intimate Account of the Revolution in English Studies at Cambridge*, p. 130.
40. *Validity in Interpretation*, p. 201 (Below, M17.)
41. "The Son of Spiders," p. 155. (Below, J29.)
42. "My Credo: Verbal Analysis," p. 597. (Below, D39.)
43. "My Credo: Verbal Analysis," p. 598.
44. Review of Lady Murasaki, *Blue Trousers*, trans. Arthur Waley; G. Rylands, *Words and Poetry*; R. Kircher, *Power and Pillars*; A. H. Gray,

Sex Relations Without Marriage; H. du Coudray, *Another Country*, p. 419. (Below, F15.)

45. "To Understand a Modern Poem," p. 61 (Below, D29.)
46. Review of Dylan Thomas, *Collected Poems* and *Under Milk Wood*, p. 636. (Below, D48.)
47. *Seven Types of Ambiguity*, p. 10.
48. "The Intentional Fallacy, Again," p. 435. (Below, G88.)
49. "The Intentional Fallacy, Again," p. 435.
50. "Introduction" to *Coleridge's Verse: A Selection*, p. 54. (Below, D88.)
51. "A Masterly Synthesis," p. 157. (Below, F46.)
52. "An American Poet," p. 521.
53. "William Empson and Categorical Criticism," p. 240. (Below, I53.)
54. "The Truest Poetrie," p. 58. (Below, J31.)
55. "Empson on Pastoral," p. 102, (Below, I2.)
56. "The Achievement of William Empson." (Below, H8.)
57. "Mr. Empson's Muddles," p. 331. (Below, I80.)
58. "Exceptional Book," p. 81. (Below, J8.)
59. *Some Versions of Pastoral*, p. 23. (Below, A2.)
60. "Empson on Pastoral," p. 101.
61. *Some Versions of Pastoral*, p. 137.
62. *Some Versions of Pastoral*, pp. 195–6.
63. *Some Versions of Pastoral*, p. 196.
64. *Some Versions of Pastoral*, p. 249.
65. *Some Versions of Pastoral*, p. 6.
66. *Some Versions of Pastoral*, p. 6.
67. *Some Versions of Pastoral*, p. 6.
68. *Some Versions of Pastoral*, pp. 4–5.
69. Brooks finds fault with this discussion of Gray, complaining that Empson has "extended the implications a little further than the total context of the whole poem warrants." "Gray's Storied Urn" (I11), p. 99.

70. *Some Versions of Pastoral*, p. 6.
71. *Some Versions of Pastoral*, p. 9.
72. *Some Versions of Pastoral*, p. 14.
73. *Some Versions of Pastoral*, p. 15.
74. *Some Versions of Pastoral*, p. 18.
75. "Early Auden," p. 33. (Below, D65.)
76. *Twentieth-Century Authors, First Supplement. A Biographical Dictionary of Modern Literature*, p. 308.
77. *The Structure of Complex Words*, p. 6. (Below, A3.)
78. *The Structure of Complex Words*, p. 7.
79. *The Structure of Complex Words*, p. 31. Sir William has told me in a letter (19 May 1983) that he no longer believes this: "This is a disgusting opinion, if one at all, and I ought to have taken care to avoid suggesting it. I meant that for a word to carry a fixed emotion presumed a firm agreement within the culture, often guiding the interpretation, and that one did not find two contrasting fixed emotions—when that seemed to happen, the feelings were mediated by Implications or Moods."
80. Review of A. V. Judges, ed., *The Elizabethan Underworld. Harman, Greene, Dekker, and Others*, p. 444. (Below, F21.)
81. "Hits and Misses," p. 673.
82. "Incomparable Empson," p. 33.
83. Richard Sleight, "Mr. Empson's Complex Words," p. 328. (Below, I90.)
84. *Style and Stylistics*, p. 91.
85. "Alice in Empsonland," p. 250. (Below, I57a.)
86. "Alice in Empsonland," p. 262.
87. *The Structure of Complex Words*, p. 418.
88. *The Structure of Complex Words*, p. 423.
89. *The Structure of Complex Words*, p. 427.
90. *The Structure of Complex Words*, p. 427.
91. *The Structure of Complex Words*, p. 427.
92. *Seven Types of Ambiguity*, p. 245.

93. This passage is worth comparing with Roland Barthes's statement that "criticism is not an homage to the truth of the past or to the truth of 'others'—it is a construction of the intelligibility of our own time." "What Is Criticism," in *Critical Essays*, trans. Richard Howard (Evanston: University of Illinois Press, 1972), p. 260.
94. "The Loss of Paradise," p. 17. (Below, G37.)
95. *Milton's God*, p. 251. (Below, A4.)
96. Alfred Alvarez, "Empson's God," p. 443. (Below, J35.)
97. Review of Roma Gill, ed., *William Empson: The Man and His Work*, p. 598. (Below, K4.)
98. "The Man within the Name: William Empson as Poet, Critic, and Friend," p. 73.
99. "More Empson than Milton?" p. 19. (Below, J47.)
100. "More Empson than Milton?" p. 20.
101. *Milton's God*, p. 133.
102. *Milton's God*, p. 116.
103. "Tantum Religio . . .," p. 209. (Below, J41.)
104. "Tantum Religio . . .," p. 211.
105. "Empson on Pastoral," p. 119.
106. "The Horrors of *King Lear*," p. 344. (Below, D37.)
107. "The Horrors of *King Lear*," p. 352.
108. "The Horrors of *King Lear*," p. 352.
109. "Falstaff and Mr. Dover Wilson," p. 246, (Below, D47.)
110. "Falstaff and Mr. Dover Wilson," p. 220.
111. "Next Time, A Wheel of Fire," p. 95. (Below, D76.)
112. "Introduction" to William Burto, ed., *Narrative Poems by Shakespeare*, p. xvi. (Below, D78.)
113. "*Volpone*," p. 651. (Below, D80.)
114. "*Volpone*," p. 666.
115. "*The Alchemist*," p. 595. (Below, D82.)
116. "*The Alchemist*," p. 596.

117. *"The Alchemist,"* p. 597.

118. See, for instance, the works listed under these headings in the bibliography that follows: D35, D54, D75, D86, D96.

119. "Rescuing Donne," p. 95. (Below, D86.)

120. "Donne and the Rhetorical Tradition," p. 578. (Below, D35.)

121. "A general return to the Grierson edition is overdue." "'There Is No Penance Due to Innocence.'" *New York Review of Books* (December 3, 1981), p. 50. (Below, D96.)

122. Review of F.A.C. Wilson, *W. B. Yeats and the Tradition*, p. 52. (Below, D61.)

123. "The Variants for the Byzantium Poems," p. 120. (Below, D71.)

124. Review of A. Norman Jeffares and K.E.W. Cross, eds., *In Excited Reverie*; Thomas Parkinson, *W. B. Yeats; The Later Poetry;* E. Malins, *Yeats and the Easter Rising*, p. 123. (Below, F88.)

125. "Joyce's Intentions," p. 27. (Below, D84.)

126. "Joyce's Intentions," p. 27.

127. "Joyce's Intentions," p. 30.

128. "The Ultimate Novel," p. 5. (Below, F99.)

129. "'Not Wrongly Moved . . .' (William Empson)," p. 194. (Below, I34.)

130. "Final Reflections," p. 312. (Below, A4d.)

131. "Introduction" to John R. Harrison, *The Reactionaries*, p. 11. (Below, D72.)

132. "Introduction" to John R. Harrison, *The Reactionaries*, p. 12.

133. "The Hammer's Ring," p. 75. (Below, D89.)

134. "The Structure of Complex Verse," p. 239. (Below, J32.)

135. "The Structure of Complex Verse," p. 239.

136. "Empson's Poetry," p. 45. (Below, I70.)

I. Primary Sources

A

BOOKS AND COLLECTIONS OF ESSAYS

A1 *Seven Types of Ambiguity*. London: Chatto & Windus, 1930. 325 pp.

For annotation, see A1b, which identifies quotations, drops a few pieces of "trivial" analysis, adds an index and a summary of chapters, makes a lot of proof corrections, includes an important preface, and generally attempts to "tidy up" A1 to produce a more satisfactory text. Empson notes, however, that "I do not think I have suppressed quietly any bit of analysis which would be worth disagreeing over" (A1b, p. vii).

A1a *Seven Types of Ambiguity*. New York: Harcourt, Brace and Co., 1931. 325 pp.

American reprint of A1.

A1b *Seven Types of Ambiguity*. 2d ed. rev. London: Chatto & Windus, 1947. xv + 258 pp.

Ch. I, The sorts of meaning to be considered; the problems of Pure Sound and of Atmosphere. First-type ambiguities arise when a detail is effective in several ways at once, e.g. by comparisons with several points of likeness, antitheses with several points of difference (p. 22), 'comparative' adjectives, subdued metaphors, and extra meanings suggested by rhythm. Annex on Dramatic Irony (p. 38). Ch. II, In second-type ambiguities two or more alternative meanings are fully resolved into one. Double grammar in Shakespeare Sonnets. Ambiguities in Chaucer (p. 58), the eighteenth century, T.S. Eliot. Digressions (p. 80) on emendations of Shakespeare and on his form 'The A and B of C.' Ch. III, The condition for third-type ambiguity is that two apparently unconnected meanings are given simultaneously. Puns from Milton, Marvell, Johnson, Pope, Hood. Generalised form when there is reference to more than one universe of discourse; allegory, mutual comparison, and pastoral. Examples from Shakespeare, Nash, Pope, Herbert, Gray. Discussion of the criterion for this type. Ch. IV, In the fourth type the alternative meanings combine to make clear a complicated state of mind in the author. Complete poems by Shakespeare and Donne considered. Examples (p. 145) of alternative possible emphases in Donne and Hopkins. Pope on dowagers praised. *Tintern Abbey* accused of failing to achieve this type. Ch. V, The fifth type is a fortunate confusion, as when the author is discovering his idea in the act of writing (examples from Shelley) or not holding it all in mind at once (examples from Swinburne). Argument that later metaphysical poets were approaching nineteenth-century technique by this route; examples from Marvell and Vaughan. Ch. VI, In the sixth type what is said is contradictory or irrelevant and the reader is forced to invent interpretations. Examples from Shakespeare, Fitzgerald, Tennyson, Herbert, Pope, Yeats. Discussion of the criterion for this type and its bearing on nineteenth-century technique. Ch. VII, The seventh type is that of full contradiction, marking a division in the author's mind. Freud invoked. Examples (pp. 198-211) of minor confusions in negation and opposition. Seventh-type ambiguities from Shakespeare, Keats, Crashaw, Hopkins, and Herbert. Ch. VIII, General discussion of the conditions under which ambiguity is valuable and the means of apprehending it. Argument that theoretical understanding of it is needed now more than previously. Not all ambiguities are relevant to criticism; example from Johnson. Discussion of how verbal analysis should be carried out and what it can hope to achieve.

Defines seven types of ambiguity (see contents above) and exploits these in a series of close readings. Explains that he will use "ambiguity" in an "extended sense, and shall think relevant to my subject any verbal nuance, however slight, which gives room for alternative reactions to the same piece of language. Sometimes ... the word may be stretched absurdly far, but it is descriptive because it suggests the analytical mode of approach, and with that I am concerned." Admits the at least partly provisional nature of the seven types: "My seven types, so far as they are not merely a convenient framework, are intended as stages of advancing logical disorder." Points out that his critical evaluations are implicit in his choices of works to discuss: "I shall almost always take poems that I admire." The passages analyzed come mainly from Shakespeare and the seventeenth-century poets.

Chapter One defends analysis against those who prize most in poetry its "Pure Sound" or its "Atmosphere." Empson's position is susceptible to summary: (1) sound should echo sense, and their relations are capable of being understood "if we knew a great deal," and our "limited knowledge ... involves much estimating of probabilities, and is less ignorance than an ordered suspension of disbelief"; (2) only bad poems are destroyed by analysis; (3) statements about Atmosphere may reflect either a sensation that is nevertheless analysable, or a synesthetic response, or--most importantly--"an undifferentiated mode of being" ("a sort of taste in the head"). For the Romantic poets, creation of Atmosphere "from a tap-root into the world of their childhood" was an escape from an "intellectual framework" that they found dispiriting.

The concluding Chapter Eight is an extremely important theoretical exploration that might profitably be read as an introduction. Several points emerge. (1) Discussion of ambiguities may shed light on the "vaguely imagined 'forces' ... essential to the totality of a poem." (2) Richards's adumbration of Sense, Feeling, Tone, and Intention is inadequate because "the process of apprehension ... is not at all like reading a list" and "makes the reader feel as two things what he must... apprehend as one thing." Empson's own method "jumps the gap between two ways of thinking" and apprehends the ambiguity "in the preconsciousness." "In the same way, there is a preliminary stage in reading poetry when the grammar is still being settled, and the words have not been given their due weight; you have a broad impression of what it is all about, but there are various incidental impressions wandering about in your mind; these may not be part of the final meaning arrived at by the judgment, but tend to be fixed in it as part of its colour." (3) On the problem of belief, Empson speaks of a "machinery of reassurance" to help "you feel that your reactions *could* be put into a rational scheme that you can roughly imagine," and adds, "To give a reassurance of this kind, indeed, is the main function of criticism." (4) "The position of a literary critic is far more a social than a scientific one. There is no question of dealing finally with the matter, because in so far as people are always reading an author, he is always being read differently. It is the business of the critic to extract for his public what it wants; to organise, what he may indeed create, the taste of his period. So that literature in so far as it is a living matter, demands a sense, not so much of what is really there, as of what is necessary to carry a particular situation 'off.'" (5) Since "The object of life, after all, is not to understand things, but to maintain one's defences and equilibrium and live as well as one can," analysis must be defended as an "appeal to the self-esteem of the readers of the analysis," who must have "defences strong enough for them to be able to afford to understand things." His own sympathies are with those Faustians "who want to understand as many things as possible, and to hang those consequences which cannot be foreseen." (6) The critic must be both appreciative and analytical. (7) Analysis comforts a reader by reassuring him that "this is all right; I am feeling correctly about this; I know the kind of way in which it is meant to be affecting me."

The preface to Alb identifies "two cross-currents" in his mind that led him away from verbal analysis: (1) the influences of Eliot and the Zeitgeist on realigning the nineteenth-century poets with Donne, Marvell, and Dryden, and (2) "the impact of Freud." It also provides a detailed response to Smith's *Criterion* review (see J7).

Alc *Seven Types of Ambiguity*. New York: New Directions, 1947. xv + 256 pp.

A reprint of Alb.

Ald *Seven Types of Ambiguity*, 3rd ed. rev. London: Chatto & Windus, 1953. xvi + 258 pp.

Includes new "Note for the Third Edition."

Ale *Seven Types of Ambiguity*. New York: New Directions, 1953. xvi + 256 pp.

American reprint of Ald.

Alf *Seven Types of Ambiguity*. New York: Noonday Press, 1955. 298 pp.

Reprint of Al.

A1g *Seven Types of Ambiguity*. Harmondsworth: Penguin Books, 1961. 256 pp.

Paperback reprint of A1b.

A1h *Seven Types of Ambiguity*. London: Chatto & Windus, 1963. xvi + 258 pp.
Reprint of A1d.

A1i *Sette tipi di ambiguita*. Edizione italiana a cura di Giorgio Melchiori. Torino: Einandi, 1965. 385 pp.

Italian translation of A1.

A1j "Ambiguity of the Fourth Type." In *The Modern Critical Spectrum,* edited by Gerald Goldberg and Nancy Goldberg. Englewood Cliffs, New Jersey: Prentice-Hall, Inc., 1962, pp. 92-108.

Reprint of A1, Ch. 4.

A1k "Ambiguities in Hopkins." In *Gerard Manley Hopkins: Poems, A Casebook,* edited by Margaret Bottrall. London: Macmillan, 1975, pp. 87-91.

Reprint of A1b, pp. 147-9 and 224-6.

A2 *Some Versions of Pastoral*. London: Chatto & Windus, 1935. 298 pp.

Ch. I, "Proletarian Literature" (D12); Ch. II, "Double Plots: Heroic and Pastoral in the Main Plot and Sub-Plot" (D9); Ch. III, "They That Have Power: Twist of Heroic-Pastoral Ideas in Shakespeare into an Ironical Acceptance of Aristocracy" (D10); Ch. IV, "Marvell's Garden: The Ideal Simplicity approached by Resolving Contradictions" (D8); Ch. V, "Milton and Bentley: The Pastoral of the Innocence of Man and Nature"; Ch. VI, "*The Beggar's Opera:* Mock-Pastoral as the Cult of Independence" (D13); Ch. VII, *Alice in Wonderland:* The Child as Swain."

Essays on widely differing works, each demonstrating a "version" of pastoral as indicated in the subtitles. The essays on Milton and Dodgson were printed here for the first time, and all of the essays are therefore annotated here for the convenience of having all the notes in one place.

"Proletarian Literature" (D12): Explores relationship between proletarian literature and the pastoral tradition: "Good proletarian art is usually Covert Pastoral"; "My own difficulty about proletarian literature is that when it comes off I find I am taking it as pastoral literature"; "Pastoral is worked from the same philosophical ideas as proletarian literature." Proletarian literature in its "wider sense" is "by the people, for the people, and about the people ... whereas pastoral though 'about' is not 'by' or 'for.'" "The essential trick of the old pastoral ... was to make simple people express strong feelings... in learned and fashionable language."

States several themes which are elaborated in the essays that follow: Gertrude Stein's work is called a "version of child-cult, which is a version of pastoral"; the Sacrificial Hero as Dying God and the pastoral figure of the Sincere Man as One with Nature interact in double plots; and the mock-pastoral derives from middle-class Puritanism.

"Double Plots: Heroic and Pastoral in the Main Plot and Sub-Plot" (D9): Part I analyzes the "mode of action" of the double plot (*Friar Bacon and Friar Bungay, Troilus and Cressida, Henry IV, Pt. I, Marriage à la Mode),* explaining that "An account of the double plot... is needed for a general view of pastoral because the interaction of the two plots gives a particularly clear setting for, or machine for imposing, the social and metaphysical ideas on which pastoral depends. What is displayed on the tragi-comic stage is a sort of marriage of the myths of heroic and pastoral, a thing felt as fundamental to both and necessary to the health of society." Part II examines examples of irony and dramatic ambiguity that grow out of double plots, "and only connected with pastoral so far as they describe a process of putting the complex into the simple."

Part III speculates on "certain magical ideas" invoked by double plots--the deification of Elizabeth, and the rise of heroic characters (e.g., Tamburlane, Faustus)--finding, for instance, in the problem of the One and the Many an analog of the relationship between the person of "magical importance" and the world he personifies: "If you choose an important member the result is heroic; if you choose an unimportant one it is pastoral."

"They That Have Power: Twist of Heroic-Pastoral Ideas in Shakespeare into an Ironical Acceptance of Aristocracy" (D10): Interprets Shakespeare's Sonnet 94 as ironical admiration for the cold, Machiavellian type who is "in some way right about life," and suggests that "its clash of admiration and contempt seems dependent on a clash of feeling about the clashes." Follows up the sonnet discussion with consideration of how the feelings in the sonnet are expressed in Angelo and Prince Henry, "different both in their power and their coldness." For these cold aristocrats of the spirit, life is seemingly inadequate, and "this grand notion of the inadequacy of life... needs to be counted as a possible territory of pastoral."

"Marvell's Garden: The Ideal Simplicity approached by Resolving Contradictions" (D8): Finds that "The Garden" reconciles "conscious and unconscious states, intuitive and intellectual modes of apprehension," through metaphorical implication. Central to this aim is Marvell's dramatization of "the mind's relation to Nature" in a poem that suggests "various interlocking hierarchies" of ideas. The couplet "Annihilating all that's made/To a green thought in a green shade" makes use, for example, of the "Hymn to David" theme of the mastery of nature through sympathetic understanding of it; and the first four verses are described as "a crescendo of wit on the themes 'success or failure is not important, only the repose that follows the exercise of one's power' and 'women, I am pleased to say, are no longer interesting to me, because nature is more beautiful.'" Several important points about pastoral are made: (1) one of its assumptions is "that you can say everything about complex people by a complete consideration of simple people"; (2)both the heroic and the pastoral "rely on a 'complex in simple' formula"; (3) "to take a simple thing and imply a hierarchy in it can then only be done in a strange world like that of Milton's Adam or a convention like that of pastoral." One important critical dictum--a seemingly deconstructionist one--is offered in the discussion of the metaphysical conceit: "I have not been able to say what machinery erects a staircase on a contradiction, but then the only essential for the poet is to give the reader a chance to build an interesting one; there are continual opportunities in the most normal use of language."

"Milton and Bentley: The Pastoral of the Innocence of Man and Nature": Discusses not only Bentley's commentary on Milton's language, but also that of Bentley's contemporary Zachary Pearce, concluding that although Milton left "a grim posterity of shoddy thinking in blank verse" and the question raised about Milton's poetry was "real," in the end "the answer justifies Milton." Defends Milton's "ornamental comparisons"--details from classical myths "used to convey very complex feelings about Paradise and also for the vilification of Eve." Concludes with the remark that "in Satan determining to destroy the innocent happiness of Eden, for the highest political motives, without hatred, not without tears, we may find some echo of the Elizabethan fulness of life that Milton as a poet abandoned, and as a Puritan helped to destroy." (See L5.)

"*The Beggar's Opera:* Mock-Pastoral as the Cult of Independence" (D13): Part I stresses the relationship between heroic and pastoral, identifying them as the "two stock halves of the double plot" because "you cannot have a proper hero without a proper people." Pastoral "describes the lives of 'simple' low people to an audience of refined wealthy people, so as to make them think first 'this is true about everyone' and then 'this is specially true about us,'" and both heroic and pastoral "assume or preach ... a proper or beautiful relation between rich and poor." The mock-hero, or rogue, is a hybrid evolved from these attitudes under the stress of Augustan politics, and he becomes a free individual independent of society: "I should say then that the essential process behind the *Opera* was a resolution of heroic and pastoral into a cult of independence."

Part II studies especially the "stock device" of double irony fostered in the play by "Comic Primness," a "trick of style" in which "the enjoyer gets the joke at both levels--both that which accepts and that which revolts against the convention that the speaker adopts primly." An important statement about pastoral is made: "It is this clash and identification of the refined, the universal, and the low that is the whole point of pastoral."

"*Alice in Wonderland*: The Child as Swain": Explains the Alice books as examples of "modern child-sentiment," involving a "shift onto the child ... of the obscure tradition of pastoral." The rogue-become-judge described in the essay on *The Beggar's Opera* is now the "child-become-judge." The device allows "covert judgments" on topical matters like evolution and progress, and has affinities with the Romantic notion that a child's intuition "contains what poetry and philosophy must spend their time laboring to recover." Abounds with penetrating observations. "To make the dream-story from which *Wonderland* was elaborated seem Freudian one has only to tell it." "The praise of the child in the Alices mainly depends on a distaste not only for sexuality but for all the distortions of vision that go with a rich emotional life." Speaking of the White Queen, "It seems clear that the *Apologia* (1864) is in sight when she believes the impossible for half an hour before breakfast, to keep in practice," and again of the White Queen: "Knitting with more and more needles she tries to control life by a more and more complex intellectual apparatus--the 'progress' of Herbert Spencer." Of the odd characters like the Mad Hatter: "It is the groundbass of this kinship with insanity, I think, that makes it so clear that the books are not trifling, and the cool courage with which Alice accepts madmen that gives them their strength."

A2a *English Pastoral Poetry*. New York: W.W. Norton, 1938. 298 pp.

American edition of A2.

A2b *Some Versions of Pastoral*. London: Chatto & Windus, 1950. 298 pp.

Second impression of A2, with errata.

A2c *Some Versions of Pastoral*. New York: New Directions, 1950. 298 pp.

Reprint of A2a.

A2d *Some Versions of Pastoral*. Harmondsworth: Penguin Books, 1966. 237 pp.

Paperback edition of A2, revised with a new preface.

A2e *English Pastoral Poetry*. Freeport, N.Y.: Books for Libraries Press, 1972. 298 pp.

Reprint of A2a.

A2f *Some Versions of Pastoral*. New York: New Directions, 1974. 298 pp.

Fourth impression of A2c, with a "Preface to the 1974 edition" by Empson.

A2g "*Alice in Wonderland*: The Child as Swain." William Phillips, ed. *Art and Psychoanalysis*. New York: Criterion Books, 1957. pp. 185-217.

Reprint of A2, pp. 253-94.

A2h "*Alice in Wonderland*: The Child as Swain." Donald Rackin, ed. *Alice's Adventures in Wonderland: A Critical Handbook*. Belmont, California: Wadsworth, 1969. pp. 240-65.

Reprint of A2, pp. 253-94.

A2i "The Child as Swain." Lewis Carroll, *Alice in Wonderland* (Norton Critical Edition), edited by Donald J.Gray. New York: W.W. Norton, 1971. pp. 337-65.

Reprint of A2, pp. 253-94.

A2j "Alice au pays de merveilles ou La Pastoral de l'enfance." Henri Perisot, ed. *Lewis Carroll*. Paris: Editions de l'Herne, 1971. pp. 173-86.

Abridgement of A2, pp. 253-94, translated by Jean Gattegno.

A2k "Alice." Robert Phillips, ed. *Aspects of Alice*. New York: Vanguard, 1971.

Reprint of A2, pp. 253-94.

A2l "Milton and Bentley: The Pastoral of the Innocence of Man and Nature." Louis L. Martz, ed. *Milton: "Paradise Lost." A Collection of Critical Essays*. Englewood Cliffs, N.J.: Prentice-Hall, Inc., 1966. pp. 19-39.

Reprint of A2, pp. 147-91.

A2m "Proletarian Literature." Eleanor Terry Lincoln, ed. *Pastoral and Romance: Modern Essays in Criticism*. Englewood Cliffs, N.J.: Prentice-Hall, Inc., 1969. pp. 61-70.

Abridgment of A2, pp. 1-23.

A3 *The Structure of Complex Words*. London: Chatto & Windus, 1951. 449 pp.

Ch. 1, "Feelings in Words" (D16); Ch. 2, "Statements in Words" (D20); Ch. 3, "Wit in the *Essay on Criticism*" (D38); Ch. 4, "All in *Paradise Lost*"; Ch. 5, "The Praise of Folly"; Ch. 6, "Fool in *Lear*" (D34); Ch. 7, "The English Dog" (D21); Ch. 8, "Timon's Dog" (D18); Ch. 9, "Honest Man" (D26); Ch. 10, "Honest Numbers"; Ch. 11, "Honest in *Othello*" (D17); Ch. 12, "Sense and

Sensibility" (D19); Ch. 13, "Sense in *Measure for Measure*" (D25); Ch. 14, "Sense in the *Prelude*" (D41); Ch. 15, "Sensible and Candid"; Ch. 16, "Mesopotamia"; Ch. 17, "Pregnancy"; Ch. 18, "Metaphor"; Ch. 19, "A is B"; Ch. 20, "The Primitive Mind"; Ch. 21, "Dictionaries"; Appendix I; Appendix II; Appendix III (D15).

The symbols below are included on the last page and constitute the "bits of machinery":

A.B the senses A and B used together

A + B the senses confused and regarded as one

A.(B) the sense B "at the back of the mind" when A is foremost

-A deliberate exclusion of Sense A from a use of the word

A/I the first Implication (or connotation) of the Sense A

A+ an appreciative pregnant sense of A, making it warmer and fuller

A- a depreciative pregnant sense

A£I the first mood of Sense A, a sentence giving the speaker's relation to someone else

among these

'A' "What I call A but they don't" or "What they do but I don't"

and

A? the Sense A used of oneself under cover of using it about someone else, or as

-A? "I am not like him"

A!I the first Emotion associated with Sense A

$\exists$A the Existence Assertion, "A is really there and worth naming"

A=B the various equations "A is B"

Empson has explained his purpose in a "Comment for Third Edition": "The basic idea is that, as the varied meanings within one word, and their interactions, are often tricky to analyse out, and yet the speakers often interpret a use of them with confidence and speed, there is likely to be an inner grammar of complex words like the overt grammar of sentences; and I tried to arrive at some of the rules." Hugh Kenner has summarized succinctly (see I57) the mechanics outlined in Chapters 1 and 2: "Doctrines are conveyed in words mainly by what Mr. Empson calls Equations; an Equation ties two senses together and implies that they have an intrinsic connection (A=B). The equations go into four classes: I: Context-meaning implies dictionary-meaning; II: Major sense implies connotation (A=A/1); III: Head-meaning implies context meaning; IV: Neither meaning can be regarded as dominant. The meaning that does the implying in the first three classes tends to be (1) more obvious; (2) less emotive; (3) narrower in range, than the one that gets implied."

Although the "bits of machinery" have not been assimilated into the analytical practices of other critics, the individual essays have been praised as stimulating explorations in the spirit of *Seven Types*. One of Empson's important aims--seen especially in Chapter 1 and in the three appendices on "Theories of Value"--is to "disentangle the Emotive from the Cognitive part of poetical language"; and in this effort he is often responding to the books of his former teacher, I.A. Richards, who is described in the dedication as "The source of all the ideas in this book, even the minor ones arrived at by disagreeing with him."

Chapters 4, 5, 10, 15, 16, 17, 18, 19, 20, 21, and Appendices I and II appear here for the first time, and therefore all the essays are annotated here for the convenience of having all the notes in the same place.

"Feelings in Words" (D16): Takes up in Part I the relationship between the Emotive and the Cognitive in language ("this interconnection is what I am trying to follow out"), rejecting Gustaf Stern's Emotive theory and finding in I.A. Richards's books a "series of phrases to the effect that the Emotions given by words in poetry are independent of their Sense"--a doctrine which, "if taken at all simply, would be sure to lead to bad criticism." Also rejects Richards's related claim "that the function of poetry is to call out an Attitude which is not dependent on any belief open to disproof by facts." Explains in Part II "my little bits of machinery" designed to give "symbols of their own to some elements often called 'feelings' in a word, which are not Emotions or even necessarily connected with emotions." Empson's "general position ... is that it would be sensible for a dictionary to recognise the Emotions in a variety of words" but that these emotions are complicated by other elements.

"Statements in Words" (D20): The title refers not to such an ordinary sense as making a statement to the press, for instance, but to the way a word may become "a sort of solid entity, able to direct opinion, thought of as like a person." Attempts to explore the nature of such words, to "codify the process of combination" of the "bits of machinery" devised in Chapter 1, and to "distinguish five ways in which a word can carry a doctrine." Points out that in the essays that follow he is chiefly interested in studying the "'key word' of a long poem, or complete play, in which the structure of meaning for the word is gradually built up," but adds that the idea "that every long poem has one key word which sums up all of it would of course be absurd."

"Wit in the *Essay on Criticism*" (D38): Offers *wit* (which appears about every sixteenth line in Pope's *Essay*) as an example of a Type I equation order, in which a word carries two meanings--one a "head" meaning, the other prompted by the context and identifying "what you are really talking about." The head meaning of *wit* in the *Essay* is 'joke': "there is not a single use of the word in the whole poem in which the idea of a joke is quite out of sight. Indeed I think the whole structure of thought in the poem depends on this." (See L18.)

"All in *Paradise Lost*": Cites *all* as an example of a word at the other extreme from the way *wit* is used by Pope. *All* in *Paradise Lost* is an "obviously important word for which an Emotive theory seems about all that you can hold."

"The Praise of Folly": Considers medieval and Elizabethan uses of *fool*, finding examples of Type IV equations in which a word has two head senses which are "identified with one another both ways round" (in this case, 'clown' and 'lunatic'), as well as other equations.

"Fool in *Lear* (D34): Close reading of *Lear* from point of view of Orwell's interpretation of it as a study of false renunciation. Empson summarizes: "Give away your lands if you want to, but don't expect to gain happiness by doing so. Probably you won't gain happiness. If you live for others, you must live for others, not as a roundabout way of getting an advantage for yourself." Throughout the play, "renunciation is examined in the light of the complex idea of folly," justifying a close look at *fool*, used forty-seven times. Concludes that the play leads to a "fundamental horror, an idea that the gods are such silly and malicious jokers that they will soon destroy the world."

"The English Dog" (D21): Studies use of *dog* in sixteenth through eighteenth centuries as one of a number of words (others mentioned are *arch, fool, rogue,* and *honest*) that picked up both patronizing and hearty slang meanings that carry "a kind of shrubbery" of what today might be called counter-culture ideas. Cites two functions for such words: "to soften the assertion of class and to build a defence against Puritanism." Discerns behind *dog* a rationalist element and a humanist one, the rationalist corresponding to the word's patronizing use, the humanist ("something vaguely anti-Christian") to its hearty use. The kind of thing Empson can do with these ideas is illustrated by this observation on Dr. Johnson: "*Tom Jones*, he thought, was wicked because it was an attempt to make the hearty dog-sentiment into a system of morality; whereas in serious talk you must keep to the rationalist one, as a sane recognition of the Old Adam." A brilliant essay.

"Timon's Dog" (D18): *Dog* explored as a double symbol in *Timon*, with Timon and Apemantus eventually exchanging the sense "in which they are dogs; Apemantus has become a flatterer and Timon a cynic."

"Honest Man" (D26): Points out and comments on the many uses of *honest* in English literature through Jane Austen.

"Honest Numbers": Takes the meanings for *honest* strained out of "Honest Man" and using the "bits of machinery" lists them as if for a dictionary.

"Honest in *Othello*" (D17): Studies the fifty-two uses of *honest* and *honesty* in *Othello*, concluding that Shakespeare "hated" the "hearty and individualist" use of the word among low people in his day and may have sensed that the word was moving toward "a sort of jovial cult of independence." By the Restoration "the word came to have in it a covert assertion that the man who accepts the natural desires, who does not live by principle, will be fit for such warm uses of *honest* as imply 'generous' and 'faithful to friends,' and to believe this is to disbelieve the Fall of Man"; but Shakespeare never uses it this way, and Iago's use of the word even involves a "rather puritanical view." Finds that "It is the two notions of being ready to blow the gaff on other people and frank to yourself about your own desires that seem to me crucial about Iago." Iago is thus not "an abstract term 'Evil'; he is a critique on an unconscious pun." Rejects Bradley's view of Othello as striving to be an absolute egoist, maintaining that "all the elements of the character are represented in the range of meanings of 'honest,' and ... the confusion of moral theory in the audience ... was symbolized or echoed in a high degree by the confusion of the word." Rejects the sympathy for emotive readings discerned in Stoll, as well as his "too frank a preference for melodrama," although admitting that "something very like a devil is what is wanted."

"Sense and Sensibility" (D19): Abstract discussion of *sense* and *sensibility*, fleshed out in the two essays on Shakespeare and Wordsworth that follow.

"Sense in *Measure for Measure*" (D25): Develops the ambiguities surrounding *sense* ('common sense' and 'sensuality') to the conclusion that "the performance with the word *sense* is made to echo the thought of the play very fully to the end."

"Sense in *The Prelude*" (D41): Observes that *sense* "comes into practically all the great passages of *Tintern Abbey* and *The Prelude* on the mind's relation to Nature," coming to mean "both the process of sensing and the supreme act of imagination," ignoring the meaning 'good sense' ("when Wordsworth has got his singing robes on he will not allow any mediating process to have occurred").

"Sensible and Candid": Discusses briefly Jane Austen's use of *sensible* and comments on the history of *candid* ("The word offers a remarkably different ideal truthteller from the *fool* as clown or the *honest* man or the *wit* or the man of *sense*").

"Mesopotamia": Instances *Mesopotamia* as a joke word with wholly emotive effects (from the old woman who "got great comfort from the blessed word Mesopotamia") and considers skeptically the notion that "In connected speech the mind is able to perform an extraordinarily complicated process of balancing and eliminating the possible resultant meanings from the interaction of these loose aggregates, and the point or purpose of the whole speech, a thing gradually discovered, is not attached to individual words."

"Pregnancy": Focuses on Hamlet's praise of his father ("He was a man, take him for all in all,/I shall not look upon his like again"), turning over the "pregnant" ("warmer and fuller") uses of *man*. One possibility offered is the "ideal man" (Type I), and a second is "man in general" (Type II).

"Metaphor": Asserts that metaphors "carry equations, if and only if they imply a pregnant use of the term for the vehicle" (Richards's tenor and vehicle are defined as 'thing meant' and 'thing said') and comments on relations between such entities as metaphors, equations, tenors, vehicles, emotive statements, pregnant words, and Mutual Metaphors (instances in which "tenor and vehicle are treated as examples of some wider concept which transcends them"). A diffuse, difficult essay.

"A is B": Part I examines gnomic phrases (e.g., God is Love, might is right) "to find whether this way of interpreting an equation is likely to leave an important meaning out or put in one which isn't there." Part II considers the implications of sentences inverted for emphasis. Part III rejects Cleanth Brooks's analysis of Keats's *Grecian Urn* ode "for not making the poem as emotional as it ought to be," but also insists that the poem's last two lines should not be read as "purely Emotive or as a fully detached bit of philosophizing."

"The Primitive Mind": Takes up the relation of false identity (identified in Chapter 2 as "a fundamental tool in the process by which we classify things") in a context of discussions of Owen Barfield's *Poetic Diction*, Piaget's *The Child's Conception of Causality*, Coomaraswamy's *Figures of Speech or Figures of Thought*, and Levy-Bruhl's *The 'Soul' of the Primitive*, finding evidence that "the use of false identity is common among primitives, as well as among ourselves." (See F30.)

"Dictionaries": Scrutinizes common dictionary practices, offering suggestions and proposing that "the interactions of the senses of a word should be included."

Appendix I: Considers implications of Stevenson's emotive view of language in *Ethics and Language* and of Richards's Theory of Value. Extremely valuable for the direct statement of Empson's conviction that it "seems quite possible to say that one decision would be *better* than another" and that "the position I am recommending is what the philosophers like to call naive realism." His fundamental orientation toward ethics and epistemology is phrased eloquently: "The creature must think 'It is good, in general, to act so as to produce good effects. Good effects are the same when I am there as when I am not, like the rest of the external world, hence they are good in you as well as in me. Hence, it is good for me to produce good effects in you.' Surely this simply follows from the intellectuality of the creature; it does not depend on exciting emotions of fraternal love or what not, though no doubt they are needed if he is to act on the belief when under strain. It is part of the process of believing that there is a real world outside you, an idea which is built up by generalisation and analogy...."

Appendix II: Reviews Morris's *Signs, Language and Behaviour*, making a sharp judgment on behaviorism: "The real trouble is not so much the doctrine as what the language always appears to be hinting--here chiefly by the word *phenomena*. It hints that if I am walking down the road and find you, a stranger, screaming under a tree-trunk, and all I have to do is push it up and let you out, then there is no meaning at all in saying that I have any obligation to let you out, or that it would be wrong not to let you out; there is no sense in my doing such a thing unless it satisfies one of my own needs."

Appendix III: Finds fault with the mechanist assumptions in Bloomfield's *Language*, admitting that acceptance of Bloomfield's argument would condemn his--Empson's--own work on complex words as "beyond the pale of the exact sciences, impossible to understand, impossible to criticize."

A4 *Milton's God*. London: Chatto & Windus, 1961. 280 pp.

Ch 1, "Critics"; Ch. 2, "Satan"; Ch. 3, "Heaven"; Ch. 4, "Eve"; Ch. 5, "Adam"; Ch. 6, "Delilah"; Ch. 7, "Christianity."

Insists emphatically on the "morally corrupting" nature of Christianity and the Christian God, and judges *Paradise Lost* as "not good in spite of but especially because of its moral confusions." As John Wain (in I101, p. 110) explains the thesis of *Milton's God*, "the strains and contradictions in *Paradise Lost* come from its being a good poem, not a bad one, since the God it sets out to justify is wicked and not justifiable." The "taste in the mind" produced by *Milton's God* is suggested by the remark that "the picture of God in the poem, including perhaps even the high moments when he speaks of the end, is astonishingly like Uncle Joe Stalin." The long final chapter on "Christianity" is a relentless, witty indictment of that religion for its "trying to patch the ancient Neolithic craving for human sacrifice on to the new transcendental God of all mankind," stressing the gloating of the blessed over the tortures of the damned: "The Christian God the Father, the God of Tertullian, Augustine and Aquinas, is the wickedest thing yet invented by the black heart of man." Much of *Milton's God* generates energy from Empson's hostility toward "Neo-Christian" critics: Hugh Kenner, C.S. Lewis, and T.S. Eliot prompt especially spirited passages.

Maintains, in Chapter 1, that Milton "probably became an Arian in the course of composition" of *Paradise Lost*. Defends Shelley's interpretation of *Paradise Lost*: "he was accepting as heroic any apparently hopeless resistance to something a man's own conscience tells him to be wrong, and I think people like C.S. Lewis are very unwise to talk as if this moral attitude was invented by the Romantics." Affirms the need to struggle "to imagine the mind of the author at the moment of composition." Derides Imagism as "nonsense." Concludes that critics often "are just accepting the position of Shelley while inventing means to evade his conclusions."

Stresses, in Chapter 2, Satan's conviction at first that God is not omnipotent. Asserts that "Milton steadily drives home that the inmost counsel of God was the Fortunate Fall of man; however wicked Satan's plan may be, it is God's plan too." Explains that Milton's devils, subject to the same dilemma as Pascal in his wager, "assume that to obey God merely out of cowardice, while his rule becomes increasingly harsh, certain that his demands are unreasonable but not that he could carry out his threats, would be gross dishonor." Describes the War in Heaven as "unusually stupid Science Fiction." Reverses himself on the claim made in *Some Versions of Pastoral* that Satan is not a consistent character. Speculates on the possible Gnostic influences on Milton's view of creation. Decides, after tracing the whole story of Satan in *Paradise Lost*, that it is a "very large-minded one."

Describes, in Chapter 3, a state of affairs in which God's omnipotence and foreknowledge make, in effect, a cruel charade of the Fall of Man: "But a parent who 'foresaw' that the children would fall and then insisted upon exposing them to the temptation in view would be considered neurotic, if nothing worse; and this is what we must ascribe to Milton's God." Discusses sympathetically--and at length--two works by M. Paul Phelps Morand: *De Comus A Satan* (1939) and *The Effects of His Political Life on John Milton* (1939). Expounds the thesis that Milton expected God to abdicate--i.e., relinquish his transcendental, anthropomorphic being and "dissolve into the landscape and become immanent only."

Proposes, in Chapter 4, that Eve thinks God actually wants her to eat the apple, "since what he is really testing is not her obedience but her courage, also whether her desire to get to Heaven is real enough to call all her courage out." Explains the dilemma Eve faces: if she eats the apple a good God will love her for her independent spirit and for having understood his intention; but if he did not want to produce an "independent-minded" Eve, "then he has behaved rather queerly, and it doesn't appear that he deserves to be obeyed"; and thus, Empson concludes, "on any hypothesis ... to eat it is probably the best thing to do."

Denies, in Chapter 5, that Adam is in the "pinch" described by C.S. Lewis, of having to choose between obedience to God and faithfulness to Eve. States the "real question": "Whether Adam was wrong to disobey him so as to share her punishment." Explains that in eating the apple Adam meant to comfort his wife "by his solidarity with her." Emphasizes the importance Milton at first attached to the doctrine of the Fortunate Fall as providing "a real justification of God," but thinks that the "glumness" of the two final books may reveal Milton's disillusionment with the Fortunate Fall as a solution.

Milton's God is Empson's most readable book. The prose is superb, the readings of Milton are close and stimulating, and the discussions of theology are unusual in literary criticism for their vigor and clarity.

A4a *Milton's God*. New York: New Directions, 1962. 280 pp.

American edition of A4.

A4b *Milton's God*. London: Chatto & Windus, 1965. 320 pp.

Revised edition of A4, corrected with notes and an appendix on "The Foisting of the Prayer into the *Eikon*" (pp. 288-318), taking up the Madan *Bibliography* of the *Eikon* and offering a hypothetical reconstruction of events that would allow for Milton's "foisting" of a fourth prayer into that work. Empson's own opinion posits an informant who tells Milton that "further inflammatory documents left by the King" are about to be circulated. "To select a prayer which could be used to make the King ridiculous, and alter it so that it could slide into acceptance among the Royalists, was a very specialized thing to do; the reason for supposing Milton did it is that we know of no other available man with that kind of skill." (See M31.)

A4c *Milton's God*. Westport, Conn.: Greenwood Press, 1978. 280 pp.

Reprint of A4a.

A4d *Milton's God*. Cambridge, London, New York: Cambridge University Press, 1981. 343 pp.

Reprint of A4. Includes "Final Reflections" (pp. 319-40), answering his critics. Clarifies his own feelings about God: "What is known of the universe so far is astoundingly wonderful and beautiful, and I am glad that I was born." Responds to critics who say that he makes Milton hate God by explaining his "main thesis" about God's high purpose: "The main story of Milton is that, though God causes much suffering, he takes no interest in it; it is merely needed for his high purpose, arrived at before the creation, of evolving a society so perfect that he may allow himself to abdicate into it." Defends himself against the "aesthete" Robson (See G71 and J43) with the contention that "Invoking real-life responses to the situation presented by a story has long been practised as a critical technique, and surely is often needed; at any rate, it is not wrong inherently."

B

BOOKS--POETRY

B1 *Poems by William Empson.* Japan: The Fox and Daffodil Press, 1934.

Fourteen poems printed for private circulation and later reprinted in B2.

B2 *Poems.* London: Chatto & Windus, 1935. viii + 48 pp.

Includes the following poems, with dates of first publication in parentheses: "The Ants" (1928 as "Sonnet"). "Value Is in Activity" (1928 as "Inhabitants"). "Invitation to Juno" (1928). "The World's End" (1928 as "Relativity"). "Rolling the Lawn" (1928). "Dissatisfaction with Metaphysics" (1928 as "Disillusion with Metaphysics"). "Poem about a Ball in the Nineteenth Century" (1927). "Sea Voyage" (1928). "To an Old Lady" (1928). "Part of Mandevil's Travels" (1928). "Camping Out" (1929). "Letter I" (1928 as "Letter"). "Letter II" (1928 as "Letter"). "Villanelle" (1928). "Arachne" (1928). "The Scales" (1930 as "Poem"). "Legal Fiction" (1928). "Sleeping Out in a College Cloister" (1929). "Earth Has Shrunk in the Wash" (1929). "Flighting for Duck" (1928). "Letter III" (1929). "This Last Pain" (1932). "Description of a View" (1930). "Homage to the British Museum" (1932). "Note on Local Flora" (1930). "Doctrinal Point" (1935). "Letter V" (1934). "Bacchus" (a verse at a time in 1933, 1935, 1937, 1940, 1942).

Also includes first publication of "Plenum and Vacuum" and "High Dive."

B2a *Collected Poems*. New York: Harcourt, Brace and Co., 1949. x + 113 pp.

American edition with a revised text and a new prefatory note. First publication of "Let It Go" and "Thanks for a Wedding Present." Includes those poems in the 1935 *Collected Poems* (B2) and *The Gathering Storm* (B3).

The final version of "Bacchus" has a complicated history. The first verse was printed in 1933 as "Bacchus"; the second verse in 1935 as "Bacchus Two"; the fifth verse in 1937 with ten more lines as "Bacchus Four"; the third verse in 1940 as "Bacchus Three"; and the fourth verse in 1942 as "Bacchus Four." (See H2, p. 151.)

B2b *Collected Poems*. London: Chatto & Windus, 1955. 119 pp.

Has a revised prefatory note, and includes "Letter IV" (1929) and first publication of "The Birth of Steel."

B2c *Collected Poems*. London: Chatto & Windus, 1956. 119 pp.

Second impression of B2b, with a supplementary prefatory note.

B2d *Collected Poems*. New York: Harcourt, Brace and Co., 1961. 119 pp.

Second American edition of B2a, corrected with additional notes, a translation of "Chinese Ballad," and "The Birth of Steel."

B2e *Collected Poems*. London: Chatto & Windus, 1962. 119 pp.

This edition contains all the poems in B2 and B3, as well as "Letter IV."

B3 *The Gathering Storm.* London: Faber & Faber, 1940. 71 pp.

Includes the following poems. Those that are being reprinted have dates of first publication in parentheses; others are printed here for the first time.

"Bacchus" (1933). "Your Teeth Are Ivory Towers." "Aubade" (1937). "The Fool." "The Shadow" (1936 as "Echo"). "The Small Bird to the Big" (1936). "Four Legs, Two Legs, Three Legs" (1935 as "Travel Note"). "Reflection from Rochester" (1936). "Courage Means Running" (1936). "Ignorance of Death." "Missing Dates" (1937). "Success" (1940 as "Poem"). "Just a Smack at Auden" (1938). "The Beautiful Train." "Manchouli." "Reflection from Anita Loos." "The Teasers" (1940). "Advice." "Anecdote from Talk." "China." "Autumn on Nan-yueh."

First printing of the complete "Bacchus," with substantial notes to the new poems.

C

BOOKS EDITED

C1 *Coleridge's Verse: A Selection.* (Co-edited with David Pirie.) London: Faber & Faber, 1972. 256 pp.

Introduction by William Empson. "To the Author of 'The Robbers.'" "Monologue to a Young Jack Ass in Jesus Piece." "The Eolian Harp." *From* "Reflections on Entering into Active Life." *From* "Religious Musings." *From* "The Destiny of Nations." "This Lime-Tree Bower My Prison." "The Foster-mother's Tale." "The Dungeon." "On a Ruined House in a Romantic Country." "The Rime of the Ancient Mariner." "Christabel." "Fire, Famine and Slaughter." "Frost at Midnight." *From* "Fears in Solitude." "The Nightingale." "Kubla Khan." "Lines Composed in a Concert-Room." "Introduction to the Tale of the Dark Ladie." "The Mad Monk." "A Letter to......." "Chamouny; the Hour Before Sunrise." "The Pains of Sleep." "Phantom." "Psyche." "Human Life." "On Donne's Poetry." "Work Without Hope." "Song." "Epitaph." "Fragments." *Textual Commentary by David Pirie. Notes by David Pirie.*

For annotation of Empson's 100-page introduction, see D88.

C1a *Coleridge's Verse: A Selection.* (Co-edited with David Pirie.) New York: Schocken, 1973. 256 pp.

A reprint of C1.

D

ESSAYS AND REVIEW ARTICLES

D1 "Ambiguity in Shakespeare's Sonnet XVI." *Experiment* No. 2 (February, 1929), pp. 3-5.

Slightly different version of *Seven Types*, pp. 54-6. Analyzes Shakespeare's Sonnet XVI as an example of the second type of ambiguity: "two or more meanings which all combine to a single mood and intention of the author."

D2 "An Early Romantic." *Cambridge Review* 50 (May 31, 1929), pp. 495-6.

Describes Vaughan as a "continual and close imitator of Herbert" who is nevertheless not at all metaphysical when at his best. Vaughan's "dreamlike or hypnotic intensity" connects him with the Romantics.

D2a "An Early Romantic." Eric Homberger, William Janeway, and Simon Schama, eds. *The Cambridge Mind*. Boston: Little, Brown; London: Jonathan Cape, 1970. pp. 252-6.

Reprint of D2.

D3 "The Sacrifice." *Experiment* No. 3 (May, 1929), pp. 41-4.

Short version of the discussion in *Seven Types*, pp. 226-33, putting forth Jesus as speaker of Herbert's poem and identifying numerous ambiguities.

D4 "Some Notes on Mr. Eliot." *Experiment* No. 4 (November, 1929), pp. 6-8.

Points out several ambiguities in Eliot's poems caused by confusion between past participles and active verbs.

D5 "' O Miselle Passer!'" *Oxford Outlook* 10 (May, 1930), pp. 470-8.

The title is from line sixteen of Catullus' poem number three and means 'Oh, poor little sparrow!'

Responds to John Sparrow's attack on Richards's *Practical Criticism* in M51. Considers Sparrow too devoted to intuitive readings. (See L32.)

D6 "Virginia Woolf." Edgell Rickword, ed. *Scrutinies* 2. London: Wishart & Company, 1931. pp. 203-16.

Admires the brilliance of Mrs. Woolf's descriptive passages, but finds these passages do not come together satisfactorily in narrative systems. The impressionist method, in which the author conveys his own attitude to things, "tries to substitute for telling a story, as the main centre of interest, what is in fact one of the by-products of telling a story."

D7 "Practical Criticism." *Oxford Outlook* 11 (March, 1931), pp. 54-7.

Continues the debate begun in D5. Provides a handy summary of his understanding of *Practical Criticism*: "Mr. Richards considers that there is no one certainly 'right' way of reading a given piece of poetry; that poetry is important because of the way it acts on people; that it does not only act valuably on the best critics; that it would be useful both for the critic and the educator to know how it acts on people; and that this can be found out (in a sufficient degree to be useful) by a process of inquiry."

D8 "Marvell's Garden." *Studies in English Literature*. English Literary Society of Japan (August, 1932).

D8a "Marvell's Garden." *Scrutiny* 1 (December, 1932), pp. 236-40.

Reprint of D8.

D8b "Marvell's Garden." *Some Versions of Pastoral* (A2), pp. 119-45.

Final, much enlarged version of D8. Annotated at A2.

D8c "Marvell's Garden." Mark Schorer, Josephine Miles, and Gordon McKenzie, eds. *Criticism: The Foundations of Modern Literary Judgment*, rev. ed. New York: Harcourt, Brace & World, 1958, pp. 342-52.

Reprint of D8b.

D8d "Marvell's Garden: The Ideal Simplicity Approached by Resolving Contradictions." Ray B.West, Jr., ed. *Essays in Modern Literary Criticism*. New York: Holt, Rinehart and Winston, 1961, pp. 335-53.

Reprint of D8b.

D8e "Marvell's Garden." Mario A.Di Cesare, ed. *George Herbert and the Seventeenth-Century Religious Poets* (Norton Critical Edition). New York: W.W. Norton, 1978, pp. 304-8.

Reprint of D8a.

D9 "The Double-Plot in *Troilus and Cressida*." *The Rising Generation* (Japan) 67 (1932), pp. 366-7, 402-3.

D9a "La double intrigue et l'ironie dans le Drame Elizabéthain." *Cahiers du Sud* 10, Numero Special (Juin, 1933), pp. 36-9.

Brief statement of the thesis first stated in D9 and developed fully in D9b.

D9b "Double Plots: Heroic and Pastoral in the Main Plot and Sub-Plot." *Some Versions of Pastoral* (A2), pp. 27-86.

Final, much enlarged version of D9. Annotated at A2.

D9c "Double Plots." Robert Wooster Stallman, ed. *Critiques and Essays in Criticism, 1920-48*. New York: Ronald Press, 1949, pp. 250-63.

Reprint of D9b.

D10 "They that have power...." *Studies in English Literature* (English Literary Society of Japan) 13 (1933), pp. 451-69.

D10a "They That Have Power: Twist of Heroic-Pastoral Ideas into an Ironic Acceptance of Aristocracy." *Some Versions of Pastoral* (A2), pp. 89-115.

Final, enlarged version of D10. Annotated at A2.

D11 "Introduction" to T.S. Eliot, *Selected Essays*, trans. T. Kitamura. Tokyo: Kinseido, 1933.

D12 "Proletarian Literature." *New English and American Literature* (Japan). (August, 1933).

D12a "Proletarian Literature." *Scrutiny* 3 (March, 1935), pp. 332-8.

Reprint of D12.

D12b "Proletarian Literature." *Some Versions of Pastoral* (A2), pp. 3-23.

Final, enlarged version of D12. Annotated at A2.

D13 "The Beggar's Opera." *The Rising Generation* (Japan) 70 (1934).

D13a "The Beggar's Opera: Mock-Pastoral as the Cult of Independence." *Some Versions of Pastoral* (A2), pp. 195-250.

Final, enlarged version of D13. Annotated at A2.

D13b "The Beggar's Opera: Mock-Pastoral as the Cult of Independence." Yvonne Noble, ed. *Twentieth-Century Interpretations of "The Beggar's Opera."* Englewood Cliffs, New Jersey: Prentice-Hall, Inc., pp. 15-41.

Reprint of 13a.

D14 Review of I.A. Richards, *Coleridge on Imagination*. *Criterion* 14 (April, 1935), pp. 482-5.

"It is easy to feel that Nature is both outside us and in some larger sense inside us, or that none of our interpretations of her are more than myths, but there is a jolt if you remember that this must apply to your landlady" (p. 483).

D15 "The Need for Translation Theory in Linguistics." *Psyche* 15 (1935), pp. 188-97.

Reprinted in A3 as "Appendix III." See annotation at A3.

D15a "Appendix III." *The Structure of Complex Words* (A3), pp. 434-43.

Reprint of D15.

D16 "Feelings in Words." *Criterion* 15 (January, 1936), pp. 183-99.

Short version of D16a.

D16a "Feelings in Words." *The Structure of Complex Words* (A3), pp. 1-38.

Final, expanded version of D16. Annotation at A3.

D17 "The Best Policy." *Life and Letters* 14 (Summer, 1936), pp. 37-45.

Almost identical with Pt. 1 of D17b.

D17a "The Best Policy." William Empson and George Garrett, eds. *Shakespeare Survey*. London: Brendin Publishing Co., 1937, pp. 5-21.

Reprint of D17.

D17b "Honest in *Othello*." *The Structure of Complex Words* (A3), pp. 218-49.

Part 1 (pp. 218-31) is an almost exact reprint of D17. Annotation at A3.

D18 "Timon's Dog." *Life and Letters* 15 (Winter, 1936), pp. 108-15.

Early version of D18b.

D18a "Timon's Dog." William Empson and George Garrett, eds. *Shakespeare Survey*. London: Brendin Publishing Co., 1937, pp. 22-36.

Reprint of D18.

D18b "Timon's Dog." *The Structure of Complex Words* (A3), pp. 175-84.

Slightly revised final version of D18. Annotation at A3.

D19 "Sense and Sensibility." *Psyche* 16 (1936), pp. 150-64.

Reprinted in A3, pp. 250-69.

D19a "Sense and Sensibility." *The Structure of Complex Words* (A3), pp. 250-69.

Reprint of D19. Annotated at A3.

D20 "Statements in Words." *Criterion* 16 (April, 1937), pp. 452-67.

Completely reworked and expanded as Chapter 2 of *The Structure of Complex Words* (A3).

D20a "Statements in Words." *The Structure of Complex Words* (A3), pp. 39-83.

Final revised and expanded version of D20. Annotation at A3.

D20b "Assertions dans le mots." André Jarry, trans. and ed. *Poétique* 6 (1971), pp. 239-70.

French version of D20.

D21 "The Phases of the English Dog" (Part I). *Life and Letters* 17 (Winter, 1937), pp. 29-36.

The first half of "The English Dog" in *The Structure of Complex Words* (A3).

D21a "The English Dog." *The Structure of Complex Words* (A3), pp. 158-74.

The first half of this essay (pp. 158-67) is a slightly revised version of D21. Annotation at A3.

D22 Review of I.A. Richards, *The Philosophy of Rhetoric*. *Criterion* 17 (October, 1937), pp. 125-9.

Complains about lack of details in exposition of the context theory of meaning; approves the use of the terms "tenor" and "vehicle." Finds the term "metaphor" to include too much in Richards's application, but at the same time says that Richards mistakenly limits metaphor to similarity, for dissimilarity, or "Disparity Action," is as "normal a basis for metaphor as likeness."

D23 "London Letter." *Poetry* 49 (1937), pp. 218-22.

Reflects on the conditions of (and for) poetry in England and America. A rejoinder to Grigson's very tart "London Letter" in *Poetry* (November, 1936), pp. 101-3. "The first or only certain reason for writing verse is to clear your own mind and fix your own feelings...." (See G28 and G29.)

D24 "The Phases of the English Dog" (Part II). *Life and Letters* 18 (Spring, 1938), pp. 36-42.

Slightly revised to become the second half of "The English Dog" in *The Structure of Complex Words* (A3).

D24a "The English Dog." *The Structure of Complex Words* (A3), pp. 158-74.

The second half of this essay is a slightly revised version of D24. Annotation at A3.

D25 "Sense in *Measure for Measure*." *Southern Review* 4 (Autumn, 1938), pp. 340-50.

D25a "Sense in *Measure for Measure*." *The Structure of Complex Words* (A3), pp. 270-88.

An expansion of D25. Annotation at A3.

D26 "Honest Man." *Southern Review* 5 (Spring, 1940), pp. 711-29.

D26a "Honest Man." *The Structure of Complex Words* (A3), pp. 185-201.

Reprint of D26. Annotation at A3.

D27 "Basic English and Wordsworth." *Kenyon Review* 2 (Autumn, 1940), pp. 449-57.

Translates the following passage into Basic and discusses key words, also comparing the early version with the late revision, preferring the early:

magnificent
The morning was, in memorable pomp,
More glorious than I ever had beheld.
The sea was laughing at a distance, all
The solid mountains were as bright as
clouds.

D28 "A Chinese University." *Life and Letters* 25 (June, 1940), pp. 239-45.

Revealing glimpse of Empson, in the disrupted war years, chatting about physics over tinned salmon and dried water beetles, as well as bathing in a pond with a water buffalo.

D29 "To Understand a Modern Poem." *Strand* (March, 1947), pp. 60-4.

A reading of Dylan Thomas's "A Refusal to Mourn the Death, by Fire, of a Child in London." Thomas works by "piling up many distant suggestions at once, and half the time is not 'saying anything' in the ordinary meaning of the term."

D29a "How to Read a Modern Poem." John Hollander, ed. *Modern Poetry: Essays in Criticism.* New York and London: Oxford University Press, 1968, pp. 243-8.

Reprint of D29.

D30 "Thy Darling in an Urn." *Sewanee Review* 55 (October, 1947), pp. 691-7.

Review of Brooks's *The Well Wrought Urn.* Of Brooks on Gray's "Elegy": "too content to find the intellectual machinery of a fine and full statement in the poem." Of Keats's "Grecian Urn": the "Beauty is Truth" passage is fine; it is "Oh Attic shape! Fair Attitude! With Brede" that is "the kind of thing that the rude and snobbish critics ... called him a Cockney for." Of Brooks's book, Empson presciently remarks that "the success seems so great that one begins to fear a new orthodoxy," but he fears it would have an "anti-emotional bias" that could make it "very arid." (See L6.)

D31 "The Structure of Complex Words." *Sewanee Review* 56 (April, 1948), pp. 230-50.

Preliminary version of Chapter 2, "Statements in Words," of A3.

D31a "Statements in Words." *The Structure of Complex Words* (A3), pp. 39-83.

Much-expanded version of D31. Annotation at A3.

D32 "Emotions in Words Again." *Kenyon Review* 10 (Autumn, 1948), pp. 579-601.

Pp. 579-92 were reprinted in *Kenyon Critics* (D42), pp. 127-37, as "Emotions in Poems." A revised version of pp. 597-601 was reprinted in *The Structure of Complex Words* (A3) as Chapter 4, "All in *Paradise Lost*." Pp. 6-15 of *Complex Words* , 3rd ed. (A3), are a reprint of the version in *Kenyon Critics* (D42).
See annotation of appropriate section of A3.

D33 "The Style of the Master." Richard Marsh and Tambimuttu, eds., *T.S. Eliot, A Symposium*. Chicago: Henry Regnery Co., 1949, pp. 35-7.

Anecdotes of Eliot.

D34 "Fool in *Lear*." *Sewanee Review* 57 (April, 1949), pp. 177-214.

See annotation at A3, where reprinted.

D34a "Fool in *Lear*." *The Structure of Complex Words* (A3), pp. 125-57.

Reprint of D34. Annotated at A3.

D35 "Donne and the Rhetorical Tradition." *Kenyon Review* 11 (Autumn, 1949), pp. 571-87.

Attacks Rosemond Tuve's argument in *Elizabethan and Metaphysical Imagery* for the importance of the rhetorical tradition in Donne's poetry, objecting that analysis of Donne's rhetoric "tends to 'explain things away.'" Maintains specifically that Donne "incessantly clashed the rhetorical claim that some individual or pair of individuals was the Logos against the new ideas of Copernicus, in the only form which made them a practical danger to theology--the idea that there is life on other planets, to which Christ presumably has not gone."

D35a "Donne and the Rhetorical Tradition." Paul J.Alpers, Jr., ed. *Elizabethan Poetry: Modern Essays in Criticism*. New York: Oxford University Press, 1967, pp. 63-77.

Reprint of D35.

D36 "A Doctrine of Aesthetics." Review of I.A. Richards, C.K. Ogden, and James Wood, *The Foundations of Aesthetics*. *Hudson Review* 2 (Spring, 1949), pp. 94-7.

A "valuable" book but regrets the authors had not been more "opinionated." "Perhaps the real test of an aesthetic theory ... is how far it frees the individual to use his own taste and judgment; it must be judged in terms of practice rather than abstract truth."

D37 "The Horrors of *King Lear*." Review of Robert B. Heilman, *This Great Stage*. *Kenyon Review* 11 (Spring, 1949), pp. 342-54.

Finds much "pietistic writing" in this study of *King Lear* and resists any "palliating of the starkness of the huge play." Rejects Heilman's case against Naturalistic readings of *Lear*, giving a blunt answer to the judgment that Cordelia and Gloucester deserve their fates: "This kind of talk from a critic always seems to me blindly inhumane; the mistake is to assume that the Aristotelian 'tragic flaw' has to be a moral fault instead of a natural limitation. But in Mr. Heilman's case there is a necessity to distribute blame in this absurd way, because he is determined to justify Nature and the gods."

D38 "Wit in the 'Essay on Criticism.'" *Hudson Review* 2 (Winter, 1950), pp. 559-77.

See annotation at A3. Also see L18.

D38a "Wit in the 'Essay on Criticism.'" *The Structure of Complex Words* (A3), pp. 84-100.

Reprint of D38.

D39 "My Credo: Verbal Analysis." *Kenyon Review* 12 (Autumn, 1950), pp. 594-601.

States clearly his own critical inclination: "There is room for a great deal of exposition, in which the business of the critic is simply to show how the machine is meant to work, and therefore to show all its working parts in turn. This is the kind of criticism I am specially interested in, and I think it is often really needed." Says of complexity as a criterion of value that one must begin with a sense that a passage is good and then consider the "profound complexities" assumed to be there, but that one should not presume a passage bad it it does not display complexity. Affirms the relevance of valuation to criticism, saying of his own practice that "to assess the value of the poem as a whole is not the primary purpose of this kind of criticism."

D40 "George Herbert and Miss Tuve." *Kenyon Review* 12 (Autumn, 1950), pp. 735-8.

Answers Miss Tuve's criticism (see M61a) of his reading of Herbert's "The Sacrifice" in *Seven Types*. Admits that he was unwise to call the poem unique and to attach to it a primal incest theme, but defends the fundamental soundness of his reading. (See F78, M27, and M62a.)

D41 "Sense in *The Prelude*." *Kenyon Review* 13 (Spring, 1951), pp. 285-302.

See annotation at A3.

D41a "Sense in *The Prelude*." *The Structure of Complex Words* (A3), pp. 289-305.

Reprint of D41.

D42 "Emotions in Poems." John Crowe Ransom, ed. *The Kenyon Critics*. Cleveland: World Publishing Co., 1951, pp. 127-37.

Reprint of D32, pp. 579-92, omitting discussion (pp. 592-601) of the mode of action of words. This version was reprinted as pp. 6-15 of *The Structure of Complex Words* (A3).

D43 "Dover Wilson on *Macbeth*." *Kenyon Review* 14 (Winter, 1952), pp. 84-102.

Rejects Dover Wilson's arguments that Shakespeare shortened *Macbeth* in an early revision, but sympathizes with an earlier dating of the first draft to put *Macbeth* after *Othello* and before *Lear*. Contends that acceptance of Dover Wilson's major thesis--"that the full play of *Macbeth* gave a much more prolonged struggle between Macbeth and his wife"--is not necessary in reaching a satisfactory interpretation.

D44 "Answers to Comments." *Essays in Criticism* 3 (1953), pp. 114-20.

Replies to several points made against him in previous issues ("I feel I get referred to with a kind of pitying fondness, as the wise old man who still doesn't know the rules which have recently been invented for the game"): (1) Defends against Kermode the value of his comparison of Marvell's "The Garden" to Buddhist philosophy; (2) discusses various points about Blake and his "dark Satanic mills," inclining to Bronowski's argument that the phrase was meant literally; (3) clarifies his meaning in several passages in *Complex Words*.

D45 "*Hamlet* When New" (Part I). *Sewanee Review* 61 (Winter, 1953), pp. 15-42.

Argues that in rewriting Kyd's *Hamlet* Shakespeare had to ward off audience cries to "Hurry up," and that his solution was to make the delay a central interest. Hypothesizes a 1600 version in which the "mystery" of Hamlet worked so well that Shakespeare spread mystery "all round" in the 1601 version.

D46 "*Hamlet* When New" (Part II). *Sewanee Review* 61 (Spring, 1953), pp. 185-205.

Assumes that the main changes in the 1601 version of *Hamlet* concern Ophelia and the Queen and suggests Hamlet may have been "too morally advanced to accept feudal ideas about revenge." Rejects Madariaga's view of Hamlet as a "cad" and denies Ophelia has already been to bed with him. "I would always sympathize with anyone who says ... that he can't put up with Hamlet at all. But I am afraid it is within hail of the more painful question whether you can put up with yourself and the race of man."

D47 "Falstaff and Mr. Dover Wilson." *Kenyon Review* 15 (Spring, 1953), pp. 213-62.

Disputes the theory that "Shakespeare made Falstaff appear in his first draft of *Henry V*, so that our present text of that play is much revised and therefore gravely confused," and sneers at Dover Wilson for "preaching at us about his Medieval Vice and his Ideal King." Attributes the theory to a need to explain away the "pathetic description" of Falstaff's death and thereby justify the "modern royalist" in his respect for Hal. Stresses the "Dramatic Ambiguity" in several parts of the Falstaff plot--such as whether the Prince is a thief and whether Falstaff killed Hotspur. Ridicules Dover Wilson's claim that Falstaff reveals a "calculated degradation." Asserts that despite his having qualities of the medieval Vice, Falstaff is more a Renaissance creation in his nationalism and Machiavellianism; and "Falstaff from his first conception was not intended to arrive at Agincourt, because the Prince was intended to reach that triumph over his broken heart."

D47a "Falstaff and Mr. Dover Wilson." G.K. Hunter, ed. *Shakespeare, "Henry IV," Parts I and II: A Casebook*. London: Macmillan, 1970, pp. 135-54.

Excerpted reprint of D47.

D48 Review of Dylan Thomas, *Collected Poems* and *Under Milk Wood*. *New Statesman* (May 15, 1954), pp. 635-6.

Resists Cyril Connolly's judgment that Dylan Thomas "distils an exquisite, mysterious, moving quality which defies analysis," saying of "Now," for example, "I assume on principle there is something there which I feel and can't see, but could see."

D48a Review of Dylan Thomas, *Collected Poems* and *Under Milk Wood*. John Malcolm Brinnin, ed. *A Casebook on Dylan Thomas*. New York: Thomas Y.Crowell, 1960, pp. 110-14.

Reprint of D48.

D48b Review of Dylan Thomas, *Collected Poems* and *Under Milk Wood*. In *Dylan Thomas: Critical Essays*. Englewood Cliffs, New Jersey: Prentice-Hall, Inc., 1966, pp. 84-8.

Reprint of D48.

D49 "Yes and No." *Essays in Criticism* 5 (January, 1955), pp. 88-90.

Brief reactions to several points made in the previous issue. (In reference, for instance, to *The Golden Bowl*: "Henry James I think was morally a very confused man.")

D50 *Twentieth-Century Authors, First Supplement. A Biographical Dictionary of Modern Literature.* Stanley Kunitz, ed. New York: H.W. Wilson Co., 1955, pp. 307-8.

Contains a useful autobiographical sketch by Empson.

D51 "Still the Strange Necessity." Review of Edmund Wilson, *The Shores of Light*; R.S. Crane, *The Language of Criticism and the Structure of Poetry*; W.K. Wimsatt, *The Verbal Icon*; and R.P. Blackmur, *Language as Gesture*. *Sewanee Review* 63 (Summer, 1955), pp. 471-9.

Praises Wilson's directness. Rejects Crane's opposition between imitative and didactic. Denies the logic of Wimsatt's Intentional Fallacy and calls the Concrete Universal a "tiresome paradox." Judges Blackmur "a great deal more humane and less off the point than these bother-headed theoretical critics."

D52 "The Theme of *Ulysses*." *Kenyon Review* 18 (Winter, 1956), pp. 26-52.

The first half of this essay (presented as a BBC Third Programme Talk on Bloomsday, 1954), asserts that "Stephen *did* go to bed with Molly, very soon after the one day of the book; and ... that Joyce when he looks back thinks it probably saved his life and anyhow made it possible for him to become the great author who tells the story." Bloom wants Stephen to sire the son he is now psychologically incapable of fathering himself. Two years later in the D52 version of this essay Empson develops as background for this theme the Ibsen-influenced plot of *Exiles*, with the explicit preparatory notes for that play: "What Joyce has in view is a startling transformation of the Eternal Triangle; from being one of the inevitable grounds of greed and aggression it becomes ... the highest or most evolved of all forms of human intimacy." In a 1962 note to the D52a reprint, Empson states, "I no longer believe that *Ulysses* describes a real event in Joyce's life at the date he gives." But he adds, "All the same, I think most of my article stands...."

D52a "The Theme of *Ulysses*." Marvin Magalaner, ed. *A James Joyce Miscellany*, third series. Carbondale: Southern Illinois University Press, 1962, pp. 127-54.

Reprint of D52, with additional note. See annotation at D52.

D53 "*The Spanish Tragedy*." *Nimbus* 3 (Summer, 1956), pp. 16-29.

Argues two main points: (1) *The Spanish Tragedy* was "simply an attempt to apply the technique and atmosphere of the *Ur-Hamlet* to the highly topical theme of the royal marriages of Spain"; and (2) Hieronymo, like Hamlet, is "both mad and not mad, both wise and not wise, and so forth."

D53a "*The Spanish Tragedy*." Derek Hudson, ed. *English Critical Essays, The Twentieth Century*, second series. London: Oxford University Press, 1958, pp. 215-35.

Reprint of D53.

D53b "*The Spanish Tragedy*." Ralph J.Kaufmann, ed. *Elizabethan Drama: Modern Essays in Criticism*. New York: Oxford University Press, 1961, pp. 60-80.

D54 "Donne the Space Man." *Kenyon Review* 19 (Summer, 1957), pp. 337-99.

Asserts that most of Donne's best love poems are informed by a wish to get to another planet, giving these poems a spirit of "adventurous freedom" and implying his rejection of Jesus' uniqueness. Realizes this argument will be rejected by most scholars but pleads that "the belief makes one much more convinced of the sincerity of his eventual conversion, and does much to clear the various accusations which have recently been made against his character." Points out that the question of life on other planets intensified the old theological dilemma regarding God's justice to man, and argues that "The young Donne, to judge from his poems, believed that every planet could have its Incarnation, and believed this with delight, because it automatically liberated an independent conscience from any earthly religious authority." Sketches the background of Bruno and others who speculated on a plurality of worlds, remarking that on this question Anglicans "were content to allow it to be more disturbing to others than to themselves." Describes Donne's position as one enabling him to keep well informed from a fairly early time on the "theology of the separate planet"; but not till he knew "the full effects of his runaway marriage" did he come to feel he was "actually planted on one." So that "By the time he took Anglican Orders ... he was thankful to get back from the interplanetary spaces." Rejects the accusation that Donne was insincere in taking Anglican Orders, leaning instead to the view that he was "one of the few men who constructed the intellectual platform from which later Anglicans felt able to behave moderately and well." Elaborates his position on various related matters: (1) Donne "habitually" incarnated some virtue in his heroes and mistresses, a practice that tended to obscure the theme of the separate planet; (2) Donne frequently depicted himself "recklessly" as a "martyr to love and thereby a founder of a religion"; (3) Donne meant what he said in the *Anniversaries*--"that the unified world picture of Catholicism had broken up"; (4) Donne may have had the kind of mystical experience characterized as an "absorption into the Absolute"; and (5) Donne was probably not a secret Catholic who felt martyred ("Surely it is much more probable, as well as more agreeable, to expect that he didn't feel committed to either sect, and saw no reason to give either of them an excuse to burn him").

After the lengthy exposition of these background matters, the theme of the separate planet is discussed as it appears in numerous poems: "The Good-Morrow," "Elegy XIX," "The Ecstasy," "Holy Sonnet V," "Air and Angels," "The Nocturnal," and "A Valediction: Forbidding Mourning." Central to many of the arguments is Empson's conviction about Donne's use of the word "sphere": "I would say that Donne started writing by giving the word *sphere* no meaning but 'Ptolemaic sphere' (though of course the basic geometrical sense of the Greek word was in regular English use), but that his successful uses of the word made it increasingly suggest to him 'planets' as a secondary meaning." Other critics (e.g., Marjorie Nicholson, Merritt Y. Hughes) are recognized throughout the essay and debated with.

D55 "*Tom Jones*." *Kenyon Review* 20 (Spring, 1958), pp. 217-49.

Maintains that Fielding deserves a larger defense than that he was "just 'essentially healthy,'" for he was preaching a "high-minded" doctrine in *Tom Jones*. Claims that "the style of Fielding is a habitual double irony" deriving from the reader's sense that Tom Jones's behavior has Fielding's covert support despite the book's "firm assertions that Tom is doing wrong," because Fielding is really maneuvering for support from both Tom's advocates and his detractors. (See Norris's comment on Empson's deconstructive intent in H6.) Fielding's "secret message" in *Tom Jones* is that "If good by nature, you can imagine other people's feelings so directly that you have an impulse to act on them as if they were your own; and this is the source of your greatest pleasures as well as of your only genuinely unselfish actions." Noble impulses are innate and suggest an "eerie likeness" to Calvin's position that we acquire good motives solely by the "sheer grace of God." Tom Jones not only has these good impulses (he has a "basic likeness to Huck Finn"), but he develops into a "real Gospel Christian." Fielding's technique of double irony is necessary to express sympathy for a society "in which many different codes of honor ... exist concurrently," and "the central purpose of reading imaginative literature is to accustom yourself to this basic fact" that different moral codes exist in the world. Criticizes the incest complication as an unrealistic "twist to make the end more exciting," unlike its "entirely justified" counterpart in *Joseph Andrews*. Speaking of the English class system, Empson defines Fielding's gentleman as one qualified to rule and judges the "liberality of spirit" Fielding attributed to high life to be "rather near to the basic virtue of having good impulses."

One of Empson's most brilliant readings. See Professor Rawson's response in I82.

D55a "*Tom Jones*." Ronald Paulson, ed. *Fielding: A Collection of Critical Essays*. Englewood Cliffs, New Jersey: Prentice-Hall, Inc., 1962, pp. 123-45.

Revised reprint of D55.

D55b "*Tom Jones*." Martin Battestin, ed. *Twentieth Century Interpretations of "Tom Jones."* Englewood Cliffs, New Jersey: Prentice-Hall, Inc., 1968.

Reprint of D55.

D55c *"Tom Jones."* Neil Compton, ed. *"Tom Jones": A Casebook*. London: Macmillan, 1970, pp. 139-72.

Reprint of D55.

D55d *"Tom Jones."* In Henry Fielding, *Tom Jones* (Norton Critical Edition), Sheridan Baker, ed. New York: W.W. Norton, 1973, pp. 869-93.

Reprint of D55.

D56 "A Defense of Delilah." *Sewanee Review* 68 (Spring, 1960), pp. 240-55.

Same as Chapter 6, *Milton's God* (A4). See annotation at A4.

D57 "The Satan of Milton." *Hudson Review* 13 (Spring, 1960), pp. 33-59.

Revised and enlarged as Chapter 2, *Milton's God* (A4). See annotation at A4.

D58 "Satan Argues His Case." *The Listener* 114 (July 7, 1960), pp. 11-13.

A "bogus problem"--Satan did *not* know he was fighting omnipotence--and he is *not* meant to be funny.

D59 "Adam and Eve." *The Listener* 114 (July 14, 1960), pp. 64-5.

Responds to critics of Milton's treatment of the fall of Eve by explaining that God is all along setting up the Fortunate Fall, which he must prevent from seeming "contemptible" and to which he must attach "all the noble errors in human history."

D60 "Heaven's Awful Monarch." *Listener* (July 21, 1960), pp. 111-14.

Argues that Milton's God must be planning to abdicate after he has created a proper universe, and observes that "Milton of course could not tell us *why* God needed to make all these characters fall before he could produce a universe so good that he could abdicate into it; that is an ultimate mystery ...." The abdication will take the form of God's being "dissolved pantheistically into the matter of the universe."

D61 Review of F.A.C. Wilson, *W.B. Yeats and the Tradition*. *Review of English Literature* 1 (July, 1960), pp. 51-6.

Rejects sharply Wilson's reading of Byzantium as Elysium, contending that the "country of the young" is Ireland. ("I do not believe that the Bosphorus has either salmon-falls or mackerel-crowded seas; it is a basic trouble about critics who revere 'symbolism' that they will not allow the literal meaning any weight at all.") Yeats is preparing for the role of "Grand Old Man," and the bird has a simple explanation: "what Yeats is saying is 'I tell you what I'll do; I'll turn myself into one of those clockwork dickey-birds, in a gilt cage.'" (See D71.)

D62 "Rhythm and Imagery in English Poetry." *British Journal of Aesthetics* 2 (January, 1962), pp. 36-54.

Points to the frequency in English of "jammed stress" (clusters of stressed syllables such as Graves called "stress-centres") and mocks the American Free Verse movement, especially as represented in William Carlos Williams: "He has renounced all the pleasures of the English language, so that he is completely American; and he only says the dullest things, so he has won the terrible fight to become completely democratic as well."

Attacks Imagism becouse "it is determinedly anti-intellectual, and tells us that we ought to try to be very stupid." (See his "revolt against symbolism" in D67.)

D63 "The Symbolism of Dickens." John Gross and Gabriel Pearson, eds. *Dickens and the Twentieth Century*. London: Routledge and Kegan Paul, 1962, pp. 13-15.

Finds a kind of symbolism in Dickens's works that is essentially theatrical.

D64 "Lady Chatterley Again." *Essays in Criticism* 13 (January, 1963), pp. 101-4.

A meditation on sexual anatomy, concluding that "in supposing Lawrence thought sodomy would be good for Connie, one is not making him inconsistent with the beliefs he had published before." (See M40.)

D65 "Early Auden." *The Review* No. 5 (February, 1963), pp. 32-4.

Praises Auden for his early poetry, calling him and Thomas "the only ones you could call poets of genius" in Empson's age. Admires the "pylon poets" of the thirties for their Socialist feelings. ("I'm very sorry I wasn't in on it".)

D66 Review of W.H. Auden, *The Dyer's Hand. New Statesman* (April 19, 1963). pp. 592-5.

Explains that in *The Enchafed Flood* (1951) Auden convinced him of the importance of the theme of maritime expansion in "The Ancient Mariner," but finds him too prone to Christian readings in *The Dyer's Hand* ("he twitters like a curate in W.S. Gilbert".)

D67 "Argufying in Poetry." *Listener* (August 22, 1963), pp. 277-90.

Repeats many of the points against Symbolism and anti-intellectualism made in D62 and defends reason in poetry: "Argufying is the kind of arguing we do in ordinary life, usually to get our own way; I do not mean nagging by it, but just a not specially dignified sort of arguing. This has always been one of the things people enjoy in poems; and it can be found in every period of English literature; but the effect of the symbolist movement is that you are forbidden to do it, with no reason given; except that the anti-intellectual movement, which has been one of the causes of symbolism, tells you that thinking is sordid and low-class. What I want to say amounts to a revolt against symbolism."

D68 *"The Ancient Mariner." Critical Quarterly* 6 (1964), pp. 298-319.

Reads "The Ancient Mariner" as an evocation of "the maritime expansion of the Western Europeans," denying that it is "an allegory in favour of redemption by torment, the central tradition of Christianity"--an interpretation which has led many critics to "the wild heights of Pecksniffery which are their spiritual home." One striking claim is that the albatross was made into a soup to ward off scurvy, "so that only the externals of the albatross were hung around the Mariner's neck later on." (See D66 and D88.)

D69 "Hunt the Symbol." *TLS* (April 23, 1964), pp. 339-41.

Expresses distaste for the Neo-Imagist readings of Shakespeare's last plays, readings reacting against the "character-mongering" of A.C. Bradley. Cites examples from D. Traversi's *Shakespeare: The Last Phase* of symbol-hunting leading to offensive moralizing, especially denying that although Shakespeare "was preparing his soul for death" while writing them, he was using the plays as a means of doing it. Identifies the "drive against character-mongering" in Shakespeare criticism with the "anti-humanist movement of Pound, Wyndham Lewis, Eliot, etc.," and asserts that "the inhumanity and wrongheadedness of the principle was bound to shine through in the end."

D70 "Mine Eyes Dazzle." Review of Clifford Leech, ed. *The Duchess of Malfi* by John Webster. *Essays in Criticism* 14 (1964), pp. 80-6.

Rejects the "ridiculous fashion" of supposing "the first audiences were jeering at the Duchess for her carnal lusts"; identifies the sensationalism of the play as stemming from the audience's perception of the "wickedness of Roman Catholic southern Europeans"; finds the moral to be "not that the Duchess was wanton but that her brothers were sinfully proud"; defends the Duchess and her husband as "reasonable and practical" in their marriage; denies that the play was meant to be a "warning against marrying a social inferior"; disagrees with critics who interpret the Duchess's last lines as an admission that she was wrong to marry Antonio ("If anything could have knocked them off their perch ... it would have been to have a modern Neo-Christian come up and say how pleased he was to find them licking the boots of the tyrant at the last, as it made a very edifying picture"); perceives in the play "a popular Dickensian moral, against the wicked rich"; assumes a "predominantly artisan" audience that would "admire aristocratic courage," "blame the family pride which destroys the lovers," and "side with their own Protestant government against wicked Spanish grandees."

D70a "Mine Eyes Dazzle." Review of Clifford Leech, ed. *The Duchess of Malfi* by John Webster. Norman Rabkin, ed. *Twentieth-Century Interpretations of "The Duchess of Malfi."* Englewood Cliffs, New Jersey: Prentice-Hall, Inc., 1968.

Reprint of D70.

D70b "Mine Eyes Dazzle." Review of Clifford Leech, ed. *The Duchess of Malfi* by John Webster. G.K. Hunter and S.K. Hunter, eds. *John Webster: A Critical Anthology*. Baltimore: Penguin Books, 1969, pp. 295-301.

Reprint of D70.

D71 "The Variants for the Byzantium Poems." R.K. Kaul, ed. *Essays Presented to Amy G. Stock*. Jaipur: Rajasthan University Press, 1965, pp. 111-36.

Rejects reading of Byzantium as Paradise or Heaven, finding in the rough drafts and in *A Vision* reason to believe Yeats had reincarnation in the real tenth-century city in mind--"a bustling and metropolitan stage" and "a possible stage towards Heaven." A stimulating discussion that concludes "the poem feels much better if one takes a waking interest in the story; there is no need to say that its merit resides in the confusion at a deep level which seems to be inherent in symbolist technique." (See D61.)

D71a "The Variants for the Byzantium Poems." *Phoenix* (Korea University), special number (1965), pp. 1-26.

Reprint of D71.

D71b "Yeats and Byzantium." *Grand Street* 1 (Summer, 1982), pp. 67-95.

Reprint of D71.

D72 "Introduction." John R. Harrison, *The Reactionaries*. New York: Schocken Books, 1967, pp. 9-12.

Calls the subjects of this book--Yeats, Lewis, Pound, Eliot, Lawrence--the "aesthetes" and identifies them with "the basic Christian tradition as enshrined in the textbooks of Unnaturalism, *Les Fleurs du Mal, A Rebours,* and *The Portrait of Dorian Gray*."

Defends Benthamism and praises Joyce for avoiding the "political and religious fashions" of Lewis and the other reactionaries.

D73 "The Phoenix and the Turtle." *Essays in Criticism* 16 (1966), pp. 147-53.

Speculates on the point of Shakespeare's praise of the Phoenix for "extinguishing its breed through 'married chastity,'" suggesting that the theme was proposed by Robert Chester. The whole book by Chester, *Love's Martyr,* which included Shakespeare's poem along with contributions from Jonson, Chapman, Marston, and others, was meant to praise Sir John Salusbury and his Lady, an "illegitimate but recognized daughter of the King of Man (or Earl of Derby)."

D74 "Literary Criticism and the Christian Revival." *The Rationalist Annual*. London: Pemberton Publishing Co., 1966, pp. 25-30.

Capsule statements of positions already developed on Donne (D54), Webster (D70), and Yeats (D71).

D74a "Literary Criticism and the Christian Revival." Karl Miller, ed. *Writing in England Today: The Last Fifteen Years*. Harmondsworth: Penguin Books, 1968, pp. 168-74.

Reprint of D74.

D75 "Donne in the New Edition." Review of Helen Gardner, ed. *John Donne: The Elegies, and the Songs and Sonnets*. *Critical Quarterly* 8 (1966), pp. 255-80.

Wants to preserve Donne's reputation as a thinker "who cast an independent eye on both Church and State," and finds Gardner's "'good' readings may easily come to mean ... those which she has been brought up to prefer." Disputes Gardner's resolution of textual cruxes in "Elegy XIX," "The Good-Morrow," "Valediction, of Weeping," "The Dream," and "The Relic," commenting that "though her information is very interesting, it does not give her enough reason to spoil the established text." Also objects to Gardner's dating of some poems in *Songs and Sonnets*, contending "that about ten of the second group need to be put back" to a date before Donne's marriage in 1601. Repeats a conviction that appears in *Seven Types* and elsewhere in his writings: "The chief benefit from reading imaginative literature is to make you realise that different people have held extremely different moral beliefs." (See G74.)

D76 "Next Time, A Wheel of Fire." Review of Maynard Mack, *"King Lear" in Our Time*. *Essays in Criticism* 17 (1967), pp. 95-102.

Expresses disappointment at Mack's "imposing an essentially medieval 'vision'" on *Lear*, eschewing any effort to "elucidate motives or excite human interest." Answers two points on which Mack had "smacked" him: (1) the remark in *Complex Words* that "no one could suppose all through a performance that Gloucester deserved to have his eyes gouged out" (Mack reproaches him here for naiveté); and (2) the observation that "Lear is mad when he says he deserves all his troubles for having begotten legitimate daughters."

D77 "Bastards and Barstards." *Essays in Criticism* 17 (1967), pp. 407-10.

Believes, with support from Kökeritz, that in Edmund's "Why Bastard?" speech in *Lear,* Shakespeare intends the two spellings of "Bastard" and "Barstadie," signifying "highborn bastards" and "common barstards." (See D79, L18, L19.)

D78 "Introduction." William Burto, ed. *Narrative Poems by Shakespeare.* New York: New American Library (Signet Classics paperback), 1968, pp. xv-xlvii.

Emphasizes the "human or experiential reality of the poems." *Venus and Adonis* is a "Myth of Origin" in which Venus is "Love walking about in person." *The Rape of Lucrece* is also a Myth of Origin: "the death of Lucrece causes an absurd change in human blood (line 1750)." *The Passionate Pilgrim* is a "cheat, by a pirate who is very appreciative of the work of Shakespeare." *A Lover's Complaint* is accepted as "evidently by Shakespeare on psychological grounds." *The Phoenix and the Turtle* (a "very good poem") is better "if viewed less portentously than has become usual."

D79 "Basstards and Barstards." *Essays in Criticism* 18 (1968), pp. 236-7.

Defends against J.C. Maxwell the point already made in D77.

D80 "*Volpone.*" *Hudson Review* 21 (Winter, 1969), pp. 651-66.

"It seems plain to me that the pietistic strain in Eng. Lit., as it has developed during the last forty years or so, regularly produces crippled or perverted moral judgments, wholly out of contact with the basic tone of feeling of the older works which they purport to interpret." Argues for indulgence in "rogue sentiment" in appreciating *Volpone,* standing prepared to "fare jovially, and clap your hands" at the end. (See D82.)

D81 "The Theme of *Ulysses*." *Twentieth Century Studies* (November, 1969), pp. 39-41.

Repeats the assertion made in D52 that Bloom invites Stephen to go to bed with Molly: "'Greater love hath no man than this,' the epic tells us, 'that a man lay down his wife for his friend.'"

D82 "*The Alchemist*." *Hudson Review* 22 (Winter, 1969--70), pp. 595-608.

Challenges the consensus he finds that "Jonson hates and despises all the characters in *The Alchemist*, either for being fools or for being knaves, because he is so moral," and asserts that we need not be "so solemn as is now usual over the repeated claims of Jonson to be an improving author." Finds that "rogue-sentiment"--affection for the "tricksters"--is fundamental to both *The Alchemist* and *Volpone*. Denies that Jonson "loathed and despised luxury" or that he felt "hatred and contempt for science." Offers a defense of Sir Epicure Mammon, Kastril, and Surly: "In the play what matters is his affection for the character; it decides the structure." Mammon is a "patron of the new sciences" and always "generous-minded"; Kastril has been badly educated but he has "splendidly good" impulses; and Surly is a "shabby gentleman," not a "petty criminal."

D83 "Dryden's Apparent Scepticism." *Essays in Criticism* 20 (1979), pp. 172-81.

Discovers in lines 311-21 of "Religio Laici" evidence of Deist convictions on the part of Dryden, who had to be subtle in his remarks "or he would lose the appearance of confuting the Deists." (See I43, G83, L14, and D91.)

D84 "Joyce's Intentions." *Twentieth Century Studies* No. 4 (November 4, 1970), pp. 26-36.

Bristles fiercely at what he calls the "Kenner Smear" (from Hugh Kenner's *Dublin's Joyce*--see F68): "The chief claim of this theory is that Stephen Dedalus is presented not as the author when young (though the book-title pretends he is) but as a possible fatal alternative, a young man who has taken some wrong turning, or slipped over the edge of some vast drop, so that he can never grow into the wise old author (intensely Christian, though in a mystically paradoxical way) who writes the book. The author nearly fell but not quite." Proceeds to prove by quotation the tenacity with which Joyce held to his antipathy for the Church, veering out of his way to take a swipe at his favorite target, the Neo-Christian "majority of Eng. Lit. critics, especially in America," whose pose is that they have "never heard of the opinions of the Enlightenment." Empson in his best slashing, polemical mood.

D85 "Orwell at the BBC." *Listener* (February 4, 1971), pp. 129-31.

Personal recollections of George Orwell, with whom Empson attended a six-week course at the BBC in 1941.

D85a "Orwell at the BBC." Miriam Gross, ed. *The World of George Orwell*. New York: Simon and Schuster, 1976, pp. 93-9.

Reprint of D85.

D86 "Rescuing Donne." Peter Amadeus Fiore, ed. *Just So Much Honor: Essays Commemorating the Four-Hundredth Anniversary of the Birth of John Donne*. University Park and London: Pennsylvania State University Press, 1972, pp. 95-148.

Regrets the passing of the twenties view "that Donne in his earlier poetry held broad and enlightened views on church and state, that he was influenced by the great scientific discoveries, and that he used the theme of freedom in love partly as a vehicle for these ideas to show what the ideological and sociological effects of Paracelsus and Copernicus would turn out to be." The Gardner edition of the love poems criticized in D75 is attacked anew and in great detail, with support drawn from Milgate's edition of the *Satires* and *Verse Letters*. In general, Empson prefers the readings of the Group V manuscripts, which he feels are treated too lightly by Gardner because "they are slovenly and full of trivial slips," and he maintains a preference for Grierson's "magnificent edition" of 1912. (See D96.)

D87 "My God Man There's Bears On It." Review of Valerie Eliot, ed. *T.S. Eliot: The Waste Land: A Facsimile and Transcript of the Original Drafts Including the Annotations of Ezra Pound. Essays in Criticism* 22 (1972), pp. 417-29.

Identifies the theme of *The Waste Land* ("which Pound intuitively recognized") as the decay and impending collapse of London. Eliot's insistence that the poem was a personal "grouse" is attributed to his bad relations with his father and the fear "that his father's prejudice was driving his wife mad." The anti-Semitic passages in the original manuscript take the place of hostility toward his father.

D88 "Introduction" to William Empson and David Pirie, eds. *Coleridge's Verse: A Selection*. London: Faber and Faber, 1972, pp. 13-100.

Scorns the Intentional Fallacy, arguing that "the editor should print the poem as it was at the fullest and most characteristic stage of its development; but he's unlikely to pick this out if he does not think about the author." Reads "The Ancient Mariner" as a work that "celebrates and epitomizes the maritime expansion of the western Europeans" and that also develops the Mariner as a "peculiarly grand case of 'Neurotic Guilt,'" specifically rejecting the interpretation of the poem as a "Christian allegory of redemption through suffering" and arguing that the Mariner is redeemed by "the return of spontaneous delight in the beauty of the world." Empson's determination to read the poet's mind emerges clearly in the explanation that in one passage "we are printing what Coleridge is not known to have written, but what he at least would have written if he had decided to keep the verse which he had long before designed for this place."

Proceeds by working backwards from the 1817 text of the "Mariner," making several points. (1) The glosses added in 1817 describe the spirits animating the corpses as angels, even though the poem does not, but they are really "Spirits of the Air." (2) The changes in the 1800 edition arose from a desire to please Wordsworth, who was annoyed by the public reaction to the "Mariner." (3) The moral of the "Mariner"--usually felt as something like "Don't pull poor pussy's tail, because God loves all his creatures"--may be regarded as a parody; "the parsonic unction was a shameful temptation, to which he eventually succumbed, but here he could use it with a clear conscience." The "real" moral was held in "reserve": "Nature is often terrible; but one should take delight in her when one's own nature allows of it; and the reward if granted is the best thing that life has to offer." (See C1, D66, D68.)

D89 "The Hammer's Ring." Reuben Brower, Helen Vendler, and John Hollander, eds. *I.A. Richards: Essays in His Honor*. New York: Oxford University Press, 1973, pp. 73-83.

Praises Richards for his Benthamite Theory of Value, affirming his own similar convictions, and reviews Richards's unsuccessful campaign for the adoption of Basic English. "A splendid career, long and various, which has brought help and enlightenment wherever it has turned."

D90 "Yeats and the Spirits." Review of Kathleen Raine, *Yeats, the Tarot, and the Golden Dawn*; and Denis Donoghue, ed. *W.B. Yeats: Memoirs, Autobiography (First Draft) and Journal*. *New York Review of Books* (December 13, 1973), pp. 43-5.

Finds Raine's discussion of the Tarot archetypes "much better than the prattle about 'imagery' now standard in academic criticism." Judges that Yeats's poetry can never "recover contact" with the "grand Renaissance philosophical turmoil" to which his movement "harked back"; and that even though he was not defeated by the spirits, "one cannot feel they were among his major successes."

D91 "A Deist Tract by Dryden." *Essays in Criticism* 25 (1975), pp. 74-100.

Argues the case for Dryden as author of a tract signed "A.W." and originally printed in *The Oracles of Reason* (1693) by Charles Blount and ascribed to Dryden in a Deist collection of 1745. Phillip Harth's *Contexts of Dryden's Thought* (1968) is drawn on extensively, although Harth's conclusions are frequently disputed. (See D83.)

D92 "Eliot and Politics." *T.S. Eliot Review* 2 (1975), pp. 3-4.

Concludes that Eliot had no politics, and then presents an engrossing summary of the life of Countess Marie Larisch, "merely glimpsed at the start of the *Waste Land*."

D93 "Natural Magic and Populism in Marvell's Poetry." R.L. Brett, ed. *Andrew Marvell: Essays on the Tercentenary of His Death*. New York: Oxford University Press for the University of Hull, 1979, pp. 36-61.

The title refers to Empson's focus on "the great Nature-poems and also the Satires, while looking for a point of contact between them." Sketches--with conjectures--Marvell's career and assumes that "The Garden" and "Upon Appleton House" were written while Marvell was with Fairfax, and takes issue with Legouis over several passages in these poems. Asserts "I think he fell in love with the Mower," and sees this event as sufficient to excite a populist sentiment. Rejects the attempt by F. Tupper to disprove Marvell's marriage. Speculates on the "communal authorship" of "Clarendon's House-Warming" and "The King's Vowes," identifying those verses he attributes to Marvell and judging them quite good.

D94 "Fairy Flight in *A Midsummer Night's Dream*." Review of Harold Brooks, ed. *A Midsummer Night's Dream* (Arden Shakespeare Series). *London Review of Books* 1 (October 25, 1979), pp. 5-8.

Takes the occasion to argue against the claim in Jan Kott's *Shakespeare Our Contemporary* (1967) that the lovers in *A Midsummer Night's Dream* have an orgy and wake up in shame ("No act of sex takes place on the fierce Night, and there is never anything to drink"). Computes Puck's speed, detecting allusions to Hariot's astronomical calculations.

D94a "Fairy Flight in *A Midsummer Night's Dream.*" Review of Harold Brooks, ed. *A Midsummer Night's Dream* (Arden Shakespeare Series). *New York Review of Books* (December, 1979), pp. b-c of supplement.

Reprint of D94.

D95 "Elizabethan Spirits." Review of Frances Yates, *The Occult Philosophy in the Elizabethan Age. London Review of Books* (April 17, 1980), pp. 1-4.

Provides broad discussion of the sixteenth-century belief in Middle Spirits, quoting C.S. Lewis's definition of "Platonism": "the doctrine that the region between the earth and the moon is crowded with airy creatures who are capable of fertile union with our own species." Questions Dame Frances Yates's refusal to include these spirits in her study of Elizabethan occultism. Points to Paracelsus in his *De Nymphis* as "The only man in the period who supports it thoroughly." Ends with praise for Dame Frances's recognition that "the B-text of *Dr. Faustus* is disgusting."

D96 "'There Is No Penance Due to Innocence.'" Review of John Carey, *John Donne: Life, Mind and Art. New York Review of Books* (December 3, 1981), pp. 42-50.

Interprets Carey as criticizing Donne's love poems because he discerns a bullying spirit in them, but claims that Carey's reading is a misinterpretation resulting from a faulty reading of "To His Mistress Going to Bed." Blames Carey's readings partly on his use of the Gardner text. Summarizes the story of the Donne manuscripts, explaining in detail his reasons for preferring the Group V texts. Rejects Carey's argument that the death of Donne's brother in Newgate stirred a hatred for Protestants in Donne. Ends with a call for a "general return" to Grierson's edition of Donne. (See D75 and D86.)

E

POEMS

E1 "Poem about a Ball in the Nineteenth Century." *Magdalene College Magazine* 8 (June, 1927), p. 111.

E1a "Poem about a Ball in the Nineteenth Century." *Experiment* No. 7 (Spring, 1931), p. 59.

Reprint of E1.

E2 "To an Old Lady." *Cambridge Review* 49 (April 20, 1928), p. 347.

E2a "To an Old Lady." C. Saltmarshe, J. Davenport, and B. Wright, eds. *Cambridge Poetry 1929*. London, 1929, p. 35.

Reprint of E2.

E3 "Sonnet." *Cambridge Review* 49 (April 27, 1928), p. 369.

Reprinted in *Collected Poems* (1955) as "The Ants."

E4 "Invitation to Juno." *Cambridge Review* 49 (May 4, 1928), p. 387.

E4a "Invitation to Juno." Michael Roberts, ed. *New Signatures*. London, 1932, p. 72.

Reprint of E4.

E5 "Rolling the Lawn." *Cambridge Review* 49 (May 4, 1928), p. 388.

E6 "Une Brioche pour Cerbère." *Cambridge Review* 49 (May 4, 1928), p. 388.

Not included in *Collected Poems.*

E7 "Relativity." *Cambridge Review* 49 (May 11, 1928), p. 406.

Reprinted in *Collected Poems* (1955), as "The World's End."

E8 "Letter." *Cambridge Review* 49 (June 6, 1928), p. 485.

Reprinted in *Collected Poems* (1955), as "Letter Two."

E8a "Letter." C. Saltmarshe, J. Davenport, and B. Wright, eds. *Cambridge Poetry 1929.* London, 1929, p. 38.

Reprint of E8.

E9 "Arachne." *Cambridge Review* 49 (June 6, 1928), p. 490.

E9a "Arachne." C. Saltmarshe, J. Davenport, and B. Wright, eds. *Cambridge Poetry 1929*. London, 1929, p. 40.

Reprint of E9.

E9b "Arachne." Alida Moore, ed. *Recent Poetry 1923-1933*. London, 1933, p. 50.

Reprint of E9.

E10 "New World Bistres." *Cambridge Review* 49 (June 6, 1928), p. 492.

Not included in *Collected Poems.*

E11 "Inhabitants." *Cambridge Review* 49 (June 6, 1928), p. 506.

Reprinted in *Collected Poems* (1955) as "Value Is in Activity."

E12 "Villanelle." *Cambridge Review* 50 (October 26, 1928), p. 52.

E12a "Villanelle." C. Saltmarshe, J. Davenport, and B. Wright, eds. *Cambridge Poetry 1929*. London, 1929, p. 37.

Reprint of E12.

E12b "Villanelle." Alida Moore, ed. *Recent Poetry 1923-1933*. London, 1933, p. 51. Reprint of E12.

E13 "Sea Voyage." *Cambridge Review* 50 (November 16, 1928), p. 131.

E14 "Legal Fiction." *Cambridge Review* 50 (November 30, 1928), p. 171.

E14a "Legal Fiction." C. Saltmarshe, J. Davenport, and B. Wright, eds. *Cambridge Poetry 1929*. London, 1929, p. 38.

Reprint of E14.

E15 "Letter." *Experiment* No. 1 (November, 1928), p. 4.

Reprinted in *Collected Poems* (1955) as "Letter One."

E15a "Letter One." Michael Roberts, ed. *New Signatures*. London, 1932, p. 66.

Reprint of E15.

E15b "Letter One." D.K. Roberts, G. Gould, and J. Lehmann, eds. *The Year's Poetry 1935*. London, 1935, pp. 92-3.

Reprint of E15.

E16 "Part of Mandevil's Travels." *Experiment* No. 1 (November, 1928), pp. 38-9.

E16a "Part of Mandevil's Travels." C. Saltmarshe, J. Davenport, and B. Wright, eds. *Cambridge Poetry 1929*. London, 1929, p. 33.

Reprint of E16.

E17 "Disillusion with Metaphysics." *Experiment* No. 1 (November, 1928), p. 48.

Reprinted in *Collected Poems* (1955), as "Dissatisfaction with Metaphysics."

E18 "Flighting for Duck." *Magdalene College Magazine* 9 (December, 1928), pp. 19-20.

E19 "Camping Out." *Experiment* No. 2 (February, 1929), p. 15.

E19a "Camping Out." Michael Roberts, ed. *New Signatures*. London, 1932, p. 71.

Reprint of E19.

E20 "Earth Has Shrunk in the Wash." *Experiment* No. 2 (February, 1929), p. 45.

E21 "Sleeping Out in a College Cloister." *Magdalene College Magazine* 9 (March, 1929), p. 46.

E21a "Sleeping Out in a College Cloister." *The Venture* No. 6 (June, 1930), p. 265.

Reprint of E21.

E22 "Insomnia." *Cambridge Review* 50 (April 19, 1929), p. 373.

Not included in *Collected Poems*.

E23 "Letter Three." *Experiment* No. 3 (May, 1929), p. 7.

E24 "Essay." *Magdalene College Magazine* 9 (June, 1929), p. 79.

Not included in *Collected Poems*.

E25 "UFA Nightmare." *Experiment* No. 4 (November, 1929), p. 28.

Not included in *Collected Poems*.

E26 "Letter Four." J. Bronowski and J. Reeves, eds. *Songs for Sixpence* No. 1. Cambridge: W. Heffer & Sons, 1929.

E26a "Letter Four." *Departure* (Oxford) 3, 9 (Spring, 1956).

Reprint of E26.

E27 "Note on Local Flora." *Experiment* No. 5 (February, 1930), p. 26.

E27a "Note on Local Flora." Michael Roberts, ed. *New Signatures*. London, 1932, p. 70.

Reprint of E27.

E27b "Note on Local Flora." *Poetica* (Japan). (January, 1932).

Reprint of E27.

E28 "Poem." *Experiment* No. 6 (October, 1930), p. 12.

Reprinted in *Collected Poems* (1955) as "The Scales."

E28a "The Scales." Michael Roberts, ed. *New Signatures*. London, 1932, p. 67.

Reprint of E28.

E29 "Description of a View." *Experiment* No. 6 (October, 1930), p.13.

E30 "This Last Pain." Michael Roberts, ed. *New Signatures*. London, 1932, p. 68.

E31 "Homage to the British Museum." *Poetica* (Japan). (January, 1932).

E32 "Bacchus." *New Verse* No. 2 (March, 1933), p. 8.

E32a "Bacchus." *The Fox and the Daffodil* (Japan) No. 5 (1934).
Reprint of E32.

E32b "Bacchus." Paul Engle and Joseph Langland, eds. *Poet's Choice*. London, 1962, pp. 85-6.

Reprint of E32.

E33 "Letter Five." D.K. Roberts, G. Gould, and J. Lehmann, eds. *The Year's Poetry 1934*. London, 1934, p. 94.

E34 "Bacchus Two." *Criterion* 14 (July, 1935), p. 572.

E35 "Travel Note." *New Verse* No. 16 (August-September, 1935), p. 9.

Reprinted in *Collected Poems* (1955), as "Four Legs, Three Legs, Two Legs."

E36 "Doctrinal Point." D.K. Roberts, G. Gould, and J. Lehmann, eds. *The Year's Poetry 1935*. London, 1935, p. 90.

E37 "Plenum and Vacuum." *Poems*. London: Chatto and Windus, 1935.

E38 "High Dive." *Poems*. London: Chatto and Windus, 1935.

E39 "Courage Means Running." *Contemporary Poetry and Prose* No. 1 (May, 1936), p. 6.

E39a "Courage Means Running." D.K. Roberts and J. Lehmann, eds. *The Year's Poetry 1936*. London, 1936, pp. 62-3.

Reprint of E39.

E40 "The Small Bird to the Big." *Listener* (August 5, 1936), p. 252.

Translated from the Japanese poem by C. Hatakeyama.

E41 "Echo." *Contemporary Poetry and Prose* No. 7 (November, 1936), p. 130.

Translated from the Japanese poem by C. Hatakeyama. Reprinted in *Collected Poems* as "The Shadow."

E42 "Reflection from Rochester." *Poetry* 49 (November, 1936), p. 68.

E42a "Reflection from Rochester." D.K. Roberts and J. Lehmann, eds. *The Year's Poetry 1936*. London, 1936, pp. 64-5.

E43 "Bacchus Four." *Poetry* 49 (January, 1937), pp. 188-9.

The fifth verse of what was to become finally "Bacchus." See annotation under B2a.

E44 "Missing Dates." *Criterion* 16 (July, 1937), p. 618.

E45 "Aubade." *Life and Letters* 17 (Winter, 1937), pp. 68-9.

E46 "Just a Smack at Auden." D.K. Roberts and Geoffrey Grigson, eds. *The Year's Poetry 1938*. London, 1938, pp. 48-50.

E47 "Bacchus Three." *Poetry* 56 (April, 1940), p. 18.

The third verse of what was to become finally "Bacchus." See annotation under B2a.

E48 "Poem." *Horizon* 1 (May, 1940), p. 315.

Reprinted in *Collected Poems* (1955) as "Success."

E49 "The Teasers." *Furioso* 1, 2 (1940), p. 13.

E50 "Your Teeth Are Ivory Towers." *The Gathering Storm*. London: Faber & Faber, pp. 17-8.

E51 "The Fool." *The Gathering Storm*. London: Faber & Faber, 1940, p. 21.

E52 "Ignorance of Death." *The Gathering Storm*. London: Faber & Faber, 1940, pp. 29-30.

E53 "The Beautiful Train." *The Gathering Storm*. London: Faber & Faber, 1940, p. 35.

E54 "Manchouli." *The Gathering Storm.* London: Faber & Faber, 1940, p. 36.

E55 "Reflection from Anita Loos." *The Gathering Storm.* London: Faber & Faber, 1940, p. 37.

E56 "Advice." *The Gathering Storm.* London: Faber & Faber, 1940, p. 39.

E57 "Anecdote from Talk." *The Gathering Storm.* London: Faber & Faber, 1940 p. 40.

E58 "China." *The Gathering Storm.* London: Faber & Faber, 1940, pp. 41-2.

E59 "Autumn on Nan-yueh." *The Gathering Storm.* London: Faber & Faber, 1940, pp. 43-54.

E60 "Bacchus IV." *Poetry* 59 (January, 1942), p. 266.

The fourth verse of what was to become finally "Bacchus." See annotation under B2a.

E61 "Sonnet" ("Not wrongly moved"). *Poetry* 59 (January, 1942), p. 266.

E61a "Sonnet" ("Not wrongly moved"). Oscar Williams, ed. *The War Poets.* London, 1945.

Reprint of E61.

E62 "Let It Go." *Collected Poems.* New York: Harcourt, Brace & Co., 1949, p. 81.

E63 "Thanks for a Wedding Present." *Collected Poems.* New York: Harcourt, Brace & Co., 1949. p. 82.

E64 "Chinese Peasant Song." *Nine* No. 9 (Summer-Autumn, 1952), p. 316.

Reprinted in *Collected Poems* (1955) as "Chinese Ballad."

E64a "Chinese Ballad." *New Statesman* (December 6, 1952), p. 683.

Reprint of E64 under new title.

E65 "The Birth of Steel." *Collected Poems*. London: Chatto and Windus, 1955, pp. 85-9.

F

REVIEWS

F1 Review of Wyndham Lewis, *Time and Western Man,* and C.E. Montagu, *Right off the Map. Granta* (October 21, 1927), p. 47.

Finds Lewis's own position not clearly stated in his "very readable" essays.

F2 Review of E.M. Forster, *Aspects of the Novel;* Richard Church, *Mood Without Measure;* and Hway-Uny, *A Chinaman's Opinion. Granta* (October 28, 1927), pp. 61-2.

Judges Forster's essays excellent but limited.

F3 Review of M. Maeterlinck, *The Life of the White Ant;* H. Wolfe, *Others Abide;* Arthur Waley, *Poems from the Greek* and *Poems from the Chinese;* E. Browne, *Poems from the Persian, Latin Anthology,* and *Poems from the Irish. Granta* (November 4, 1927), p. 89.

F4 Review of T.S. Eliot, ed. *The Monthly Criterion,* Nos. 1-5; G.K. Chesterton, *The Secret of Father Brown. Granta* (November 11, 1927), pp. 104-5.

Praises *The Criterion* for its debate on intuition that "cleared up some intuitionist foolishness."

F5 Review of Aldous Huxley, *Proper Studies;* Mark VII, *A Subaltern on the Somme. Granta* (November 18, 1927), p. 123.

Laments a "pseudo-Catholic bias" he finds in Huxley.

F6 Review of Logan Pearsall Smith, *The Prospects of Literature;* and *Oxford Poetry 1927. Granta* (November 25, 1927), p. 154.

F7 Review of O. Sitwell and S. Sitwell, *All at Sea;* Wyndham Lewis, *The Wild Body;* J. Hillyer, *Reluctantly Told;* R.J.S. M'Dowall, ed., *Mind;* P.A. Thompson, *Lions Led by Donkeys;* A.C. Benson, *Cressage;* and D. Pye, *George Leigh Mallory, a Memoir. Granta* (December, 2, 1927), pp. 192-4.

The Sitwell book is marred by a "long, megalomaniac introduction"; the result of putting together the *Mind* essays is a "very low organism indeed."

F8 Review of J.B.S. Haldane, *Possible Worlds;* C.L. Whyte, *Archimedes, or the Future of Physics;* and Sir A. Shipley, *Hunting Under the Microscope. Granta* (January 27, 1928), p. 229.

F9 Review of "The Janitor," *The Feet of the Young Men;* T. Le Breton, *Mr. Teedles, the Gland Old Man;* and L. Ward, *Condemnation of the Action Française. Granta* (February 3, 1928), p. 250.

F10 Review of John Dryden, *King Arthur: A Dramatic Opera;* T.W. Jones, *Hermes, or the Future of Chemistry;* J.R. Bond, *et al., British Farmers in Denmark;* and R.H. Platt, *The Book of Opportunities. Granta* (February 17, 1928), pp. 285-6.

F11 Review of B. Goolden, *The Sleeping Sword;* and *The Monthly Criterion,* Vol. 7, Nos. 1-2. *Granta* (February 24, 1928), p. 304.

F12 Review of Thornton Wilder, *The Bridge of San Luis Rey;* C.N. Williamson, *Hollywood Love;* E.C. Middleton, *Potiphar's Wife;* H. Acton, *Cornelian: A Fable;* H.R. Wakefield, *They Return at Evening;* Sir A. Quiller-Couch, *A Lecture on Lectures;* and M.C. Sturge, *Opposite Things. Granta* (March 9, 1928), pp. 339-40.

"When Mr. Wilder takes his subject seriously he is magnificent; but he is continually exploiting his style to make an escape from his subject into whimsicality." *Cornelian* is "pretty dim stuff." On Quiller-Couch's book: "Lectures are suited to a display of personality and of mental trapeze-work; so that lecturers on English and mathematics, at any rate, have some chance of putting up a fairly good music-hall show."

F13 Review of A. Weigall, *Flights into Antiquity;* C. Pendrill, *Wanderings in Medieval London;* E. Scott, *War Among Ladies;* B. Mowshay, *Fraudern Bear;* H.G. Wells, *The Way the World Is Going;* C.E. Playne, *The Pre-War Mind in Britain;* D. Pitt, *Sweeney Todd, the Demon Barber of Fleet Street;* W. Gerhardie, *Jazz and Jasper;* J. Agate, *Gemel in London. Granta* (April 27, 1928), pp. 375-6.

"Mr. Wells leaves a great deal out, but he has obviously something to say...."

F14 Review of *The Eugenics Review. Granta* (May 4, 1928), p. 396.

F15 Review of Lady Murasaki, *Blue Trousers,* trans. Arthur Waley; G. Rylands, *Words and Poetry;* R. Kircher, *Power and Pillars;* A.H. Gray, *Sex Relations Without Marriage;* H. du Coudray, *Another Country. Granta* (May 11, 1928), pp. 419-20.

The Genji novel is "done supremely here"; of the Rylands book: "The Robert Graves' school of criticism is only impressive when the analysis it employs becomes so elaborate as to score a rhetorical triumph; when each word in the line is given four or five meanings, four or five reasons for sounding right and suggesting the right things."

F16 Review of J.W. Dunne, *An Experiment with Time. Cambridge Review* (May 25, 1928), pp. 446-7.

F17 Review of K. Capek, *How a Play Is Produced;* E. Fleg, *The Boy Prophet. Granta* (May 25, 1928), pp. 457-8.

F18 Review of H.G. Wood, *Why Mr. Bertrand Russell Is Not a Christian;* W.F. Harvey, *The Beast with Five Fingers. Granta* (June 1, 1928), pp. 481-2.

F19 Review of P. Mairet, *ABC of Adler's Psychology;* R. Macaulay, *Keeping Up Appearances;* A.J. Brown, *Four Boon Fellows. Granta* (June 8, 1928), pp. 519-22.

F20 Review of Sherard Vines, *Triforium. Cambridge Review* (November 23, 1928), p. 161.

F21 Review of A.V. Judges, ed. *The Elizabethan Underworld. Harman, Greene, Dekker, and Others. The Nation & Athenaeum* (July 5, 1930), p. 444.

Makes a comment that looks ahead to *The Structure of Complex Words:* "Since that time our stress on the complexity of words in themselves has increased, so that a single word has come to be thought of as a complex molecule which must not be unpacked in ordinary use...."

F22 Review of Elizabeth Holmes, *Studies in Elizabethan Imagery. Criterion* 9 (July, 1930), pp. 769-74.

Illuminates his own views on writing criticism in criticizing Holmes's style for faults that are "becoming endemic in contemporary intellectualism." Maintains that in quoting, appreciative criticism is acceptable in establishing your authority, and figurative language is proper in producing a "literary effect similar to the one you wish to isolate from the passage;" but in critical remarks "you must not work by metaphor and suggestion but state your result as plainly (in as transferable, intellectually handy terms) as you can."

F23 Review of E.A. Burtt, *The Metaphysical Foundations of Modern Science. Criterion* 10 (October, 1930), pp. 167-71.

Rejects Burtt's thesis that "the early scientists drained the real world of spirituality unnecessarily" and judges his attitude as "not mathematical enough to repair the bases of physics." A non-mathematical analysis based on "psychoanalytical rather than religious terms" would be preferable.

F24 Review of recent poetry: P.P. Graves, "The Pursuit"; G.K. Chesterton, "The Grave of Arthur"; Robinson Jeffers, "Dear Judas"; Richard Church, "The Glance Backward"; Roy Campbell, "The Gum Trees"; T.S. Eliot, "Marina." *The Nation & Athenaeum* (February 21, 1931), p. 672.

"'Marina' seems to me one of Mr. Eliot's very good poems."

F25 Review of Katherine M. Wilson, *Sound and Meaning in English Poetry*. *Criterion* 10 (April, 1931), pp. 529-34.

"... certainly work on pure sound is a very valuable adjunct to criticism, so long as it is not taken for criticism itself."

F26 Review of Ernest Mackey, *The Indus Civilization*. *New Statesman* (April 27, 1935), p. 592.

Observes apropos of the Harappa and Mohenjodaro sites, that "It is splendid, and a piece of good luck, that so much has been discovered about early civilisation, but we are not likely to discover the really interesting things."

F27 Review of George Barker, *Poems*. *New Statesman* (May 18, 1935), pp. 720-2.

Remarks in a sympathetic review that "the poet is perhaps of all artists the least helped by advice, so the large part of criticism which amounts to covert advice is more impertinent than usual."

F28 Review of I.A. Richards, *Basic Rules of Reason* and *Basic in Teaching*. *Spectator* (June 14, 1935), pp. 1024-6.

Gives a brief account of Basic and several reasons for its importance.

F29 Review of John Laird, *An Enquiry into Moral Notions*. *Spectator* (November 29, 1935), p. 912.

F30 Review of J. Steward Lincoln, *The Dream in Primitive Cultures*. *Spectator* (January 10, 1936), pp. 64-6.

Reveals keen interest in the psychoanalytical study of dreams in primitive cultures. See "The Primitive Mind" in A3.

F31 Review of J.W. Bews, *Human Ecology*. *Spectator* (January 27, 1936), p. 103.

F32 Review of G.K. Zipf, *The Psycho-Biology of Language*. *Spectator* (February 14, 1936), p. 270.

F33 Review of Harry Price, *Confessions of a Ghost Hunter*. *Spectator* (April 10, 1936), p. 675.

F34 Review of Sir Leonard Woolley and T.E. Lawrence, *The Wilderness of Zin*; and Sir Leonard Woolley, *Abraham*. *Spectator* (April 17, 1936), p. 714.

F35 Review of David Daiches, *The Place of Meaning in Poetry*; and P. Gurrey, *The Appreciation of Poetry*. *Criterion* 15 (April, 1936), pp. 518-21.

Defends "The Waste Land" against Daiches' charge that it makes "no attempt at communication."

One observation stands out in the Gurrey review: "No doubt it's good for teachers to be harried, and the only practical advice is negative; what is wanted from them is tolerable good taste, power to convey gusto without seeming funny, and room to do it."

F36 Review of Geoffrey Gorer, *Bali and Angkor*. *Spectator* (May 8, 1936), p. 844.

F37 Review of J.W. Friend and J. Feibleman, *The Unlimited Community*. *Spectator* (August 7, 1936), p. 246.

F38 Review of C.S. Lewis, *The Allegory of Love*. *Spectator* (September 4, 1936), p. 389.

Provides a judgment that many will agree with on "the real use of the book for a general reader": "It gives an effective account of works whose beauty and reality for us we need to recognise, and yet which, in all willingness, nobody who simply likes a good book can read."

F39 Review of E.G. Boulenger, *Apes and Monkeys;* Lorna Lewis, *Jubilee and Her Mother;* Dr. Bastian Schmid, *Interviewing Animals;* and J. Morewood Dowsett, *Animal Life of Yesterday and Today. Spectator* (October 30, 1936), pp. 766-8.

F40 Review of U. Nisbet, *The Onlie Begetter;* G. Wilson Knight, *Principles of Shakespearean Production;* and F.A. Yates, *A Study of "Love's Labour's Lost." Life and Letters* 15 (Autumn, 1936), pp. 201-4.

Accepts Nisbet's claim that William Herbert of Red Castle is a "plausible candidate" for Mr. W.H., even though the evidence is "slight." (See F83.) Judges *Principles of Shakespearean Production* inferior to Knight's previous books and disagrees with his satisfaction in "ordinary performances." Praises Yates's study for the picture it develops of the intellectual atmosphere of Shakespeare's day, but dismisses the biographical speculations.

F41 Review of A.S. Cairncross, *The Problem of "Hamlet." Life and Letters* 15 (Winter, 1936), pp. 210-11.

Rejects the argument that *Hamlet* was written in 1588-89.

F42 Review of A.E. Housman, *More Poems. Poetry* 49 (1937), pp. 228-31.

Praises "this narrow and haunting poetry." "But it is the only poetry I have yet seen having a pernicious effect on the young."

F43 Review of Lord Raglan, *The Hero. Life and Letters* 16 (Spring, 1937), pp. 155-6.

Rejects the thesis that heroic figures like King Arthur originated in primitive cultures.

F44 Review of D.G. James, *Scepticism and Poetry;* David Daiches, *New Literary Values;* Dallas Kenmare, *The Future of Poetry;* Martin Gilkes, *Introduction to Modern Poetry;* and Bhawani Shankar, *Modern English Poetry. Criterion* 10 (July, 1937), pp. 705-7.

"A careful study of these books leads one to agree rather solemnly with what they so often tell us, that to write good criticism is very hard indeed. In fact some kinds of error are best avoided if you just jump at the thing."

F45 Review of F. Aveling, *Psychology: The Changing Outlook;* C.S. Myers, *In the Realm of the Mind. Spectator* (August 20, 1937), pp. 324-5.

F46 "A Masterly Synthesis." Review of Cleanth Brooks, *Modern Poetry and the Tradition. Poetry* 55 (1939), pp. 154-7.

Objects that "Truth" is something "which Mr. Brooks wants to keep out of poetry." Brooks offers a "cast-iron program, and it makes for a healthy toughness in critics, but I can't see that it goes all the way."

F47 Review of Madam Chiang Kai-Shek, *China and Peace and War. Spectator* (March 15, 1940), p. 386.

F48 Review of F.S. Boas, *Christopher Marlowe. Life and Letters* 26 (August, 1940), pp. 173-5.

Calls Boas's literary criticism "flabby."

F49 Review of G.M. Young, ed., *Selected Poems of Thomas Hardy. New Statesman* (September 14, 1940), pp. 263-4.

Admits irritation with Hardy for the "same complacence which could be satisfied with a clumsy piece of padding to make a lyric out of a twaddling reflection." Complains about Young's selections, such as the following about the World Will from *The Dynasts:*

Heaving dumbly
As we deem
Moulding numbly
As in dream.

Empson's comment on this passage is crushing: "How the very hindquarters of the bewildered mammoths loom through the bog! The words echo in the mind, as we critics say, rumbling humbly in a team or stumbling tumbly to a gleam."

F50 Review of M. Prawdin, *The Mongol Empire*. *Life and Letters* 27 (October, 1940), pp. 51-3.

"The whole claim for the Noble Savage (that important myth) was that he had a free mind, like Jenghis between the four great religions (though the nomad sentiment was always closest to Islam)."

F51 Review of William York Tindall, *D.H. Lawrence and Susan His Cow*. *Horizon* 2 (December, 1940). pp. 344-6.

Announces that this is a "repulsive little book." Objects to the study of Lawrence's reading and the "neat hints" that his ideas were "stolen." "Lawrence was a comic if you like, but he was a man of very wide and intelligent reading, in several languages, who did not choose to live near a public library: there's nothing more to say about that."

F52 Review of A.J. Ayer, *The Foundations of Empirical Knowledge*. *Horizon* 3 (March, 1941), pp. 222-3.

Calls this "an excellent book," but won't accept "that we can only build up our knowledge out of what our senses give." Several of Empson's comments are provocative: "Tennyson believed in immortality because his heart felt it, evidently sense-datum of visceral type. Sense-data become opinions rather than perceptions." Also, in speaking of matter: "How are we better off by reducing it to sense-data, which we can't perceive ourselves as having?"

F53 Review of Ida Pruitt, *A Daughter of Han*; and John F. Embree, *A Japanese Village*. *New Statesman* (June 29, 1946), p. 477.

F54 Review of Kathleen Raine, *The Year One*. *New Statesman* (November 1, 1952), p. 518.

Gives these poems a generally favorable notice.

F55 Review of Donald Davie, *Purity of Diction in English Verse*. *New Statesman* (December 13, 1952), p. 724.

Concedes the value of much of this study, but cautions that "Nobody seems to understand these changes of feeling about sound--my own are merely those of my generation--and it seems at least premature to erect a moral theory on the current ones."

F56 Review of S.J. Kahn, *Science and Aesthetic Judgement*; and Herbert Read, *The True Voice of Feeling*. *New Statesman* (March 21, 1953), pp.343-4.

Questions Sir Herbert's support for Jungian and Imagist notions, finding them corollaries of the untenable "Jam Theory" ("we have all human experience inside us, simply as the jam in our tin").

F57 "An American Poet." Review of Wallace Stevens, *Selected Poems*. *Listener* (March 26, 1953), p. 521.

Gives a generally favorable review, but laments some of the "new fancy dress" in the language. "One can't help wishing he had found more to say, if only because he evidently could say it."

F58 Review of Basil Davidson, *Daybreak in China*. *New Statesman* (June 20, 1953), p. 750.

F59 Review of Joseph Bertram, *Conscience and the King*; and Jean Paris, *Hamlet ou Les Personnages du Fils*. *New Statesman* (October 3, 1953), p. 380.

F60 Review of Frank Moraes, *Report on Mao's China*; and Raja Hutheesing, *Window on China*. *Listener* (October 8, 1953), pp. 595-6.

F61 Review of George Whalley, *Poetic Process*; and W.J. Entwistle, *Aspects of Language*. *New Statesman* (October 31, 1953), p. 530.

F62 Review of V. de S. Pinto, ed. *Poems by John Wilmot, Earl of Rochester*. *New Statesman* (November 28, 1953), pp. 691-2.

Sympathizes with problems of understanding Rochester: "It took a number of pretty wild characters to create the placid and apparently unbreakable world of the eighteenth century."

F63 "The Pride of Othello." Review of G.R. Elliott, *Flaming Minister*. *Kenyon Review* 16 (Winter, 1954), pp. 163-6.

Takes issue with the thesis that *Othello* is a dramatization of the evils of pride.

F64 Review of James Cameron, *Mandarin Red*. *Listener* (June 9, 1955), p. 1039.

F65 Review of S. Hanayama, *The Way of Deliverance*. *New Statesman* (September 17, 1955), pp. 337-8.

Comments on this account of the prison lives of Japanese war criminals under sentence of death. The author is the Buddhist priest who attended them.

F66 Review of Robert Graves, *The Crowning Privilege*. *New Statesman* (October 1, 1955), pp. 400-2.

Identifies Graves as one of the founders of modern literary criticism, but rejects his Jungian convictions.

F67 Review of I.A. Richards, *Speculative Instruments*; and John Wain, ed. *Interpretations*. *New Statesman* (December 10, 1955), pp. 799-800.

F68 "Humanism and Mr. Bloom." Review of Hugh Kenner, *Dublin's Joyce*. *New Statesman* (August 11, 1956), pp. 163-4.

Expresses the same objections as in D84. "Now I think that to read Joyce like this, as solely concerned to jeer at all human affections, is to make him a very disgusting author.... To have a critic in sympathy with this frame of mind does not make it any more agreeable."

F69 Review of James Bertram, *Return to China*; and Robert Guillain, *The Blue Ants*. *New Statesman* (November 2, 1957), pp. 573-4.

F70 Review of Ellsworth Mason and Richard Ellman, eds. *The Critical Writings of James Joyce*. *New Statesman* (June 20, 1959), p. 868.

Describes this volume as useful mainly in supporting the view that Joyce never weakened in his opposition to the Church.

F71 Review of Richard Ellman, *James Joyce*. *New Statesman* (October 31, 1959), pp. 585-6.

"It is a grand biography," but "using the notes and index is made like climbing a ten-foot wall with broken bottles on it." Admits that *Ulysses* seems less autobiographical to him after reading this biography, "but all the same what the novel *Ulysses* is really about cannot be thought clear from the biography." See D84, where he argues for the existence of an "Ur-Molly."

F72 Review of Leslie Hotson, *Shakespeare's Wooden O*. *New Statesman* (February 13, 1960), pp. 224-5.

Equivocal review. "The truth is that the Elizabethans ... are tiresomely bad at simple description; it is irritatingly hard luck that we can't decide how Shakespeare meant his plays to be acted...."

F73 Review of J.B. Broadbent, *Some Graver Subject: An Essay on "Paradise Lost."* *Listener* (August 4, 1960), p. 196.

F74 "Professor Lewis on Linguistics." Review of C.S. Lewis, *Studies in Words*. *TLS* (September 30, 1960), p. 627.

Debates Lewis on "wit" (see A3), which Empson had claimed was identified in Pope with the modern sense of "smart joker." "Professor Lewis proves that the word was habitually used when Pope wrote to mean the highest powers of the human mind."

F75 Review of John Peter, *A Critique of "Paradise Lost." Listener* (October 27, 1960), pp. 750-2.

A book of "vigorous good sense." Rejects Peter's reading of IV, 50, as evidence that God let only half the good angels go to fight the angels.

F76 Review of Arthur Koestler, *The Lotus and the Robot. New Statesman* (January 6, 1961), pp. 21-2.

Comments wittily on Koestler's analysis of Zen and Yoga, chiding him for giving aid and comfort to Christianity but admitting that "the exposure of Yoga was needed."

F77 "Shakespeare and Dover Wilson." Review of J. Dover Wilson, *Shakespeare's Happy Comedies. New Statesman* (December 7, 1962), pp. 827-8.

Accepts all of Dover Wilson's arguments for Shakespeare's revisions except his conclusions about *Twelfth Night*.

F78 Review of T.S. Eliot, *George Herbert. New Statesman* (January 4, 1963), p. 18.

Renews his quarrel with R. Tuve over Herbert's "The Sacrifice." (See D40 and M62a.)

F79 "The Age of the Telly." Review of Marshall McLuhan, *The Gutenberg Galaxy. Universities Quarterly* 17 (March, 1963), pp. 203-4.

Expresses relief that "the people envisaged were only viewers of the telly." The book is "a picture of the coming age which Wyndham Lewis for one ... had given long before with vomiting horror."

F80 Review of Christopher Ricks, *Milton's Grand Style. New Statesman* (August 23, 1963), p. 230.

"Milton is a larger poet than he appears in this book, but it brings out some of his more astonishing technical powers, and it refutes a lot of talk against him which has been influential for a generation."

F81 Review of Martin Seymour-Smith, ed. *Shakespeare's Sonnets;* A.L. Rowse, *William Shakespeare;* and Peter Quennell, *Shakespeare. New Statesman* (October 4, 1963), pp. 447-8.

Seymour-Smith makes Shakespeare "very 'contempry'"; inclines to agree with Rowse in rejecting a sodomistic relationship between Shakespeare and Southampton.

F82 Review of H.W. Piper, *The Active Universe. Critical Quarterly* 5 (1963), pp. 267-71.

Inconclusive discussion of the Romantics' belief in animate nature. (See D68.)

F83 Review of J. Dover Wilson, *Shakespeare's Sonnets. New Statesman* (February 7, 1964), pp. 216-7.

Rejects Dover Wilson's thesis that the sonnets were addressed to William Herbert ("I am a Southampton man myself"). (See F40.)

F84 Review of Arthur Waley, *The Secret History of the Mongols. New Statesman* (March 13, 1964), p. 410.

F85 Review of Leslie Hotson, *Mr. W.H. New Statesman* (April 24, 1964), p. 642.

Sceptical of the claim that the Sonnets were written to William Hatcliffe, a law student at Gray's Inn.

F86 Review of D.P. Walker, *The Decline of Hell. New Statesman* (August 21, 1964), p. 248.

F87 Review of Francis Berry, *The Shakespearean Inset. New Statesman* (June 18, 1965), pp. 966-7.

Expresses doubt about Berry's definition of an inset as an episode in which "the imagined spectacle is at odds with the actual spectacle" ("I think the superstition of Imagism is at its fell work"), arguing that what Berry really has in mind is like what Joyce meant by epiphany.

F88 Review of A. Norman Jeffares and K.E.W. Cross, eds. *In Excited Reverie*; Thomas Parkinson, *W.B. Yeats: The Later Poetry*; and E. Malins, *Yeats and the Easter Rising*. *New Statesman* (July 23, 1965), pp. 123-4.

Spends essentially the whole review in commenting on Conor Cruise O'Brien's essay on Yeats's politics in the Jeffares-Cross volume, pointing out that Yeats shared his Fascist beliefs with "all the great writers in English in the first half of this century, except Joyce." Insists Yeats should not be regarded as "part of a world line-up with Hitler." Complains about the suppression in the Yeats centenary writings of the poet's central belief in reincarnation: "The refusal to recognize it in Yeats's poems often makes nonsense or gives a bad meaning."

"Mr. Parkinson's book is written in a very foreign language, the high guff of US Eng Lit which can only be read by angels...."

F89 Review of Constantine Fitzgibbon, *The Life of Dylan Thomas*. *New Statesman* (October 29, 1965), pp. 647-8.

Believes that Thomas would soon have had relief from money matters, and "Probably we would be learning very different moral lessons from his career if the obituaries were appearing now."

F90 Review of Helen Gardner, *A Reading of "Paradise Lost." New Statesman* (December 24, 1965), p. 1004.

Defends his own method of close reading of *Paradise Lost* against Gardner's rejection of it in this book of "immense blandness."

F91 Review of Northrop Frye, *Five Essays on Milton's Epics*. *Listener* (July 28, 1966), p. 137.

"I am glad not to have to believe in the Milton of Professor Frye and his individualist herd, as he would be a nasty character."

F92 Review of S.G.F. Brandon, *The Judgement of the Dead*. *Listener* (November 30), 1967, p. 709.

F93 Review of Brigid Brophy, *Black and White: A Study of Aubrey Beardsley*. *Listener* (November 28, 1968), pp. 721-2.

Finds Brophy's psychological analysis sympathetic but irrelevant and tending to obscure the likable side of Beardsley.

F94 "Some More Dylan Thomas." Review of Walford Davies, ed. *Dylan Thomas: Early Prose Writings*; and Daniel Jones, ed. *Dylan Thomas: The Poems*. *Listener* (October 28, 1971), pp. 588-90.

Concludes that the prose volume contains some wonderful pieces, but that there is not much new in the book of poems. Says of "Altar-wise by owl light" ("the most obscure of Dylan Thomas's poems") that it was a misguided attempt at writing Symbolist poetry, a "lethal theory" which he dropped, "and we must thank his wonderful powers of recovery for releasing him from it."

F95 "The Voice of the Underdog." Review of Wayne C. Booth, *A Rhetoric of Irony*. *The Journal of General Education* 26 (Winter, 1975), pp. 335-41.

Judges this a "good book," but feels the definition of irony given should be narrowed.

F96 "Reading the Epic of Gilgamesh." *The Journal of General Education* 27 (Winter, 1976), pp. 241-54.

Discusses the two editions, in 1964 and 1972, of N.K. Sandars' translation of *Gilgamesh*, praising it especially for trying to stay close to the original ("it is better not to read translations at all than read doctored 'contemporized' ones"). Glosses various aspects of *Gilgamesh*: parallels to Shelley's "Adonais," evidence of a pantheist view of Nature, Gilgamesh's ancestry. Observes that "The desire to find some kind of relation between civilized man and wild Nature ... lies at the root of the whole story," and claims that "odd though it may seem, this really is the guilt of man in the poem--polluting the environment."

F97 "Compacted Doctrines." Review of Raymond Williams, *Keywords: A Vocabulary of Culture and Society*. *New York Review of Books* (October 27, 1977), pp. 21-2.

Admits the fairness of Williams's account of different meanings interacting in a word to form "compacted doctrines" (which sound like Empson's own complex words), but the words chosen for review make clear Empson's lack of sympathy for Williams's left-wing ideology. Describes Williams's theories as "terribly waffle," leaving him "free to choose any interpretation that suits his own line of propaganda."

F98 "Advanced Thought." Review of Frank Kermode, *The Genesis of Secrecy*. *The London Review of Books* 2, 1 (January 24, 1980), pp. 1-3.

Interprets this book as claiming that "no history or biography can be believed, but must be regarded as a kind of novel," and thinks that using examples from the Gospels is "rather unfair" because of the special problems raised by the miracles. Argues that Kermode "gets into nonsense" by not reading his key passages as deliberate fiction: "he will not imagine a 'character' who makes a literary quotation on purpose, and hearers who know he is doing it." Even though he is sceptical of the ability of Kermode and "the rest of his school" to interpret novels, he praises Kermode's final chapter on the mystery of the Gospel for its "incessant glimmering of the unapprehensible."

F99 "The Ultimate Novel." Review of Hugh Kenner, *Ulysses;* and E.L. Epstein, ed. *A Starchamber Quiry: A James Joyce Centennial Volume 1882-1982*. *London Review of Books* (August 19-September 2, 1982), pp. 3-5.

Rejects Kenner's idea that Stephen is almost blind all through *Ulysses,* and also denies that Molly has been pure all through the ten years of no sex with her husband. Argues vigorously the thesis that Joyce, who "would have wanted to present a real modern marriage" and had himself considered (but found he couldn't tolerate) a love triangle, wanted to leave a "real and challenging" question at the end of whether Stephen will return. Attacks the "Wimsatt Law," which forbids this kind of speculation. Scorns the attempt by Robert Boyle SJ, in the *Quiry*, to show that Joyce made his peace with Christianity: "He would also think it a betrayal to twist his writings into propaganda for the worship of the torture-monster." Also denies that *Ulysses* opposes contraception.

G

MISCELLANEOUS

G1 Reviews of films. *Granta* (May 6, 1927), p. 410; (May 13, 1927), p. 430; (May 20, 1927), p. 438; (May 27, 1927), p. 463; (June 10, 1927), p. 522; (October 14, 1927), p. 18; (November 4, 1927), pp. 84-5.

G2 Humorous verse and prose sketches (with J.H.E.P. Marks). *Granta* (November 18, 1927), p. 116.

G3 Reviews of films and plays. *Cambridge Review* (April 27, 1928), p. 375; (May 4, 1928), p. 396; (May 25, 1928), p. 452; (June 6, 1928), p. 513; (October 19, 1928), pp. 33-4.

G4 Reviews of films and plays. *Granta* (October 19, 1928), p. 42; (October 26, 1928), p. 63; (November 9, 1928), p. 111; (November 16, 1928), p. 120; (November 23, 1928), p. 154; (November 30, 1928), p. 197.

G5 Letter to Desmond Flower. *Cambridge Review* 49 (May 11, 1928), pp. 412-3.

G6 Humorous verse and prose sketches. *Granta* (February 3, 1928), p. 243; (November 2, 1928), pp. 74, 85; (November 16, 1928), p. 123; (November 30, 1928), p. 180; with J.H.E.P. Marks (October 12, 1928), p. 8.

G7 Review of J. Van Druten, *Diversion* (a play). *Cambridge Review* (March 8, 1929), p. 355.

G8 Reviews of films. *Granta* (February 1, 1929), p. 262; (May 3, 1929), p. 420.

G9 Humorous prose sketch (with J.H.E.P. Marks). *Granta* (March 8, 1929), p. 352.

G10 "Shelley." (Letter in reply to Edmund Blunden's review of *Seven Types of Ambiguity.*) *The Nation and Athenaeum* (November 29, 1930), p. 291.

G11 "A Note on W.H. Auden's 'Paid on Both Sides.'" *Experiment* No. 7 (Spring, 1931), p. 60.

G12 "Learning of English." *Japan Chronicle* (November 25, 1931).

G13 "Harold Monroe." *The Rising Generation* (Japan) 67 (1932), p. 151.

G14 "Mrs. Dalloway." *The Rising Generation* (Japan) 67 (1932), pp. 182-3.

G15 "A Comparative Experiment in Text Simplification" (Pandora and the Box put into Basic). *The Bulletin of the Institute for Research in English* (Japan), No. 88 (October-November, 1932), pp. 6-8.

G16 "Basic English." *Japan Chronicle* (August 17, 1932).

G17 "T.E. Hulme's *Speculations.*" *The Rising Generation* 69 (1933), pp. 2-3.

G18 Letter on "An Experiment in Text Simplification." *Bulletin of the Institute for Research in English Teaching* (Japan), No. 90 (January, 1933), pp. 3-4.

G19 Letters "Concerning 'Basic English.'" *Bulletin of the Institute for Research in English Teaching* (Japan), No. 91 (February, 1933), p. 2; No. 92 (March, 1933), p. 7; No. 96 (July, 1933), p. 7; No. 98 (October-November, 1933), p. 10.

G20 "Words with Meaning." *Japan Chronicle* (February 23, 1933).

G21 "Notes on 'Arachne.'" *The Rising Generation* (Japan) 70 (1934).

G22 "On the Teaching of Literature," tran. S. Narita. *Literary Art* (Japan), 1934.

G23 Letter "Concerning 'Basic English.'" *Spectator* (August 2, 1935), p. 191.

G24 Letter concerning a review of *Some Versions of Pastoral* in the previous issue. *TLS* (December 7, 1935), p. 838.

"My only claim is so little is known about the action of language that one can fairly look round for 'all possible' ways in which the agreed effect may have been produced."

G25 Translation into "Basic" of J.B.S. Haldane, *The Outlook of Science* (Psyche Miniatures). London: K. Paul, Trench, Trubner & Co., 1935.

G26 Translation into "Basic" of J.B.S. Haldane, *Science and Well-Being* (Psyche Miniatures). London: K. Paul, Trench, Trubner & Co., 1935.

G27 "The Faces of Buddha." *Listener* (February 5, 1936), pp. 238-40.

Empson's book manuscript on this subject was lost during the war.

G28 "About Grigson." *Poetry* 49 (January, 1937), p. 237.

Sharply disparages Grigson for his "trick of being rude to everybody."

G29 "Reply to Grigson." *Poetry* 50 (May, 1937), p. 116.

Answers Grigson's sneer (see K8) about Empson's criticism with the observation that "it is a bad thing to be a quarter-man, but it is a great sign of being a quarter-man if you strut about squaring your shoulders and seeing how rude you can be."

G30 "Ballet of the Far East." *Listener* (July 7, 1937), pp. 16-8.

Explains the difference between Eastern and Western ballet in terms of theology: "In the West, the supreme God is a person, in the East he is not; their ideas about man follow from that, and you come across examples of it all the time."

G31 "Passing Through U.S.A." *Horizon* 1 (June, 1940), pp. 425-30.

Gives his impressions of American press propaganda regarding the wars in Europe and Asia, based on a three-month stay in America while traveling home from China in late 1939.

G32 "Did You Hear That?" *Listener* (January 1, 1942), p. 9.

Remarks on Japanese students.

G33 "These Japanese." *Listener* (March 5, 1942), 293-4, 309.

Interesting personal observations about the Japanese national character. "Unfortunately they have taken it into their heads to be the rulers of a great Asiatic empire. Now that's the last thing they're any good at."

G34 Letter on "The Staging of *Hamlet*." *TLS* (November 23, 1951), p. 749.

G35 "This is a good block." *TLS* (December 19, 1952), p. 837.

Letter on a textual point in *King Lear*.

G36 "Bare Ruined Choirs." *Essays in Criticism* 3 (July, 1953), pp. 357-8, 362-3.

Defends himself against F.W. Bateson's criticism (see I4) of his discussion in *Seven Types* of the "bare ruined choirs" in Shakespeare's Sonnet LXXIII.

G37 "The Loss of Paradise." *The Northern Miscellany of Literary Criticism* No. 1 (1953), pp. 17-18.

States here the idea that eight years later became central to *Milton's God*: that the "startling irreducible confusions" in *Paradise Lost* "so far from proving that the poem is bad, explain *why* it is so good."

G38 "Empson, Adams, and Milton." *Partisan Review* 21 (November-December, 1954), pp. 699-700.

Letter in reply to Adams's article (see I1) pointing out the misquotations in his essay on Bentley and Pearce's editing of Milton. Denies that his account of *Paradise Lost* could have done any harm ("But I wasn't telling anybody how to read it ...").

G39 Letter on Hopkins's "Windhover." *TLS* (October 1, 1954), p. 625.

G40 Letter on the Elizabethan stage. *TLS* (December 10, 1954), p. 801.

G41 Autobiographical sketch. Stanley Kunitz, ed. *Twentieth Century Authors, First Supplement. A Biographical Dictionary of Modern Literature.* New York: H.W. Wilson Co., 1955, pp. 307-8.

G42 Letter on Hopkins's "Windhover." *TLS* (May 20, 1955), p. 269.

G43 Letter on masques. *The Times* (June 13, 1955), p. 9.

G44 Letter in reply to Geoffrey Strickland's article on Empson's criticism. *Mandrake* 2 (Autumn-Winter, 1955-56), pp. 47-8.

Defends the sincerity of *Complex Words*. Retorts with a *tu quoque*: "I think it an 'alarming portent', to borrow a stock phrase of this school, when I come home and find sheer platoons of pompous young men, each of them mouthing and leering and insinuating and displaying his donnish 'intimacy' in precisely the same manner, a manner into which he has been drilled. Wherever the eye hits, on any page written by one of these indistinguishable young men, it receives an immediate impression of farcical insincerity." (See I94.)

G45 "Mr. Empson and the Fire Sermon." *Essays in Criticism* 6 (October, 1956), pp. 481-2.

Explains, in answer to Rodway's query in J32, why he included a version of the Fire Sermon at the beginning of his *Collected Poems,* clarifying that he is not dedicated to Buddhism: "Of course I think Buddhism much better than Christianity, because it managed to get away from the neolithic craving to gloat over human sacrifice; but even so I feel it should be applied cautiously, like the new wonder-drugs."

G46 Letter on *Waiting for Godot. TLS* (March 30, 1956), p. 195.

G47 "Restoration Comedy Again." *Essays in Criticism* 7 (July, 1957), p. 318.

G48 "On the 'Fire Sermon.'" *Arrows* (Sheffield University student magazine). New Year 1957 edition, pp. 5-6.

G49 "Great Writers Rediscovered. The Grandeur of Fielding's *Tom Jones.*" *Sunday Times* (March 30, 1958), p. 13.

G50 Letter on *Paradise Lost. TLS* (October 3, 1958), p. 561.

A reply to F.R. Leavis

G51 Letter on George Orwell's *1984. Critical Quarterly* 1 (Summer, 1959), pp. 157-9.

Argues that Orwell thought the worst thing about Communism was its similarity to Christianity.

G52 Letter on "Christianity and *1984.*" *Critical Quarterly* 1 (Winter, 1959), p. 352.

Defends the thesis of G51. See G.S. Fraser's comment in L9.

G53 *Listen*, LPV3, *William Empson Reading Selected Poems*. With sleeve notes on the poems by W.E. London: Marvel Press, 1959.

A gramophone record.

G54 Letter concerning broadcasts on *Milton's God*. *Listener* (July 28, 1960), p. 157. (See D58, D59, and D60.)

G55 Letter on *The Muse in Chains*. *TLS* (August 5, 1960), p. 497.

See the annotation of Tillyard's book at M58.

G56 Letter on "Academic Caste." *TLS* (April 28, 1961), p. 263.

G57 Letter on *King Lear*. *Critical Quarterly* 3 (Spring, 1961), pp. 67-8.

Clarifies his point (see A3) about Lear's death, that he was supporting Orwell's view about Lear's "still cursing, still not understanding anything" at the end.

G58 Letter on R.L. Brett's review of *Milton's God*. *Critical Quarterly* 3 (Winter, 1961), p. 368.

Explains further his understanding of Milton's view of the claim of the identity of the Father and the Son: "he makes the Father and the Son about as identical as a terrier and a camel."

G59 Letter on a review of *Milton's God*. *TLS* (October 6, 1961), p. 663.

Defends the relevance of *Milton's God* and his position that a poem is not a "private self-subsisting world."

G60 "Pei-Ta Before the Siege." *Arrows* (Sheffield University student magazine). (1959-61), pp. 6-8.

G61 Letters regarding Milton's *Eikonoklastes*. *TLS* (March 2, 1962), p. 137; (March 23, 1962), p. 201; (April 27, 1962), p. 281; (May 25, 1962), p. 380.

See A4, appendix to A4b, and M31.

G62 "Dylan Thomas." *Essays in Criticism* 13 (April, 1963), pp. 205-7.

Defends Thomas's poetry against the criticism made by David Holbrook in *Llareggub Revisited*: "it is absurd to denounce poets who find a mystical beauty in the child's delight and wonder at the new-made world."

G63 Conversation with Christopher Ricks. *The Review* Nos. 6 and 7 (June, 1963), pp. 26-35.

Talks mostly about his poetry: "The first book, you see, is about the young man feeling frightened, frightened of women, frightened of jobs, frightened of everything, not knowing what he could possibly do. The second book is all about politics, saying we're going to have this second world war and we mustn't get too frightened about it." Excellent interview.

G63a Conversation with Christopher Ricks. Ian Hamilton, ed. *The Modern Poet: Essays from "The Review."* London: MacDonald, 1968, pp. 177-87.

Reprint of G63.

G64 "Resurrection." *Critical Quarterly* 6 (1964), p. 83.

Disputes John Wren-Lewis's claim that an act of faith in the resurrection of the body would encourage "a revolution in ethics." (See G65 and L35.)

G65 "Resurrection." *Critical Quarterly* 6 (1964), p. 178.

Comments on John Wren-Lewis's reply in L35 to G64.

G66 "A Theoretical Point." In *John Crowe Ransom: Gentleman, Teacher, Poet, Editor, Founder of 'The Kenyon Review.' A Tribute from the Community of Letters*, ed. D. David Long and Michael R. Burr. Supplement to *The Kenyon Collegian*, 90, 7 (1964), p. 36.

Explains how he was at first put off by Ransom's

distinction between "structure" and "texture" but later came to see the "good sense" of Ransom's position.

G67 "The Ogden Portrait of Shakespeare." *New Statesman* (October 9, 1964), p. 550.

"There is room for doubt about the origins of the Ogden portrait, but as a face it is the only one which allows itself to be believed in."

G68 "Shakespeare's Characters." *Critical Quarterly* 7 (1965), p. 285.

Expresses scorn for two dogmas: that the reader must not know anything outside the text, and "that a poet only expresses himself in Images, so that there *couldn't* be two different characters in a poetic drama." (See L30 and M36.)

G69 Comments on the Symposium "The Living Language." *TLS* (January 14, 1965), p. 32.

Asks about the age and origin of such locutions as "He said to shut the window."

G70 Comments on the Symposium "The Living Language." *TLS* (May 27, 1965), p. 437.

Asserts that "Writers can do a good deal towards the upkeep of the language."

G71 Reply to James Jensen in I54. *Modern Language Quarterly* 27 (1966), pp. 257-8.

Reviews his early relationship with Richards, denying any instruction from Richards on *Seven Types*. "Robert Graves had used the method of analysis by recognising ambiguity in a previous book, not collaborating with anyone; I ran into an irrelevant difficulty merely by quoting the wrong book." (See L11 and L15.)

G72 Letter in reply to W.W. Robson's review of *Milton's God*. *Oxford Review* No. 3 (Michaelmas, 1966), pp. 77-9.

Explains, apropos of why Eve ate the apple,

that "when she decides to eat, she believes what Satan has just told her, that God wants her to eat the apple, since he is testing not her obedience but her courage, and the sincerity of her desire to go to Heaven." (See A4b and J46.)

G73 Letter on "*Macbeth* in History." *The Times* (October 25, 1966), p. 13.

Regards *Macbeth* as a "Just-So Story" about the Scots accepting the "more civilized hereditary principle."

G74 Letter on Donne. *Critical Quarterly* 9 (1967), p. 89.

Explains that Professor Gardner has given him information about two of the Donne textual cruces he discussed in the Autumn, 1966, issue of *Critical Quarterly* and confesses his conjectures were "thus very ridiculous," but defends his arguments as a whole. (See D75.)

G75 Letter on *Troilus and Cressida*. *TLS* (March 2, 1967), p. 167.

Argues that *Troilus and Cressida* was written for the Globe. Rejects the notion that Ajax is a caricature of Ben Jonson. (See G76 and G77.)

G76 Letter on *Troilus and Cressida*. *TLS* (April 6, 1967), p. 296.

Speculates that the title page of the 1609 quarto of *Troilus and Cressida* was altered because the editor found out that by not performing the play the Company had lost its right to forbid publication. (See G75 and G77.)

G77 Letter on *Troilus and Cressida*. *TLS* (April 20, 1967), p. 340.

Dismisses the hypothesis that Shakespeare's company published a quarto of *Troilus and Cressida* that has not survived. (See G75 and G76.)

G78 Interview with William Empson. *The Star* (Sheffield), (March 31, 1967), p. 64.

G79 Letter concerning "The Achievement of William Empson," by Roger Sale. *Hudson Review* 20 (1967), pp. 534-8.

"He finds there is a paltry side to Empson; naturally enough, as he has been taught to expect it in all mankind. It is my happy duty to relieve him here.... Empson is pure where he stands accused; the consequences of the Fall are to be found only among his traducers. Surely this will admit a gleam of sunlight into the Calvinist underworld." (See L29.)

G80 Contributions to a broadcast talk about J.B.S. Haldane. *Listener* (November 2, 1967), pp. 565-8.

G81 Letter on Swinburne and D.H. Lawrence. *TLS* (February 20, 1969), p. 185.

Gives examples of what he likes in Swinburne; ranks Dylan Thomas somewhat higher than Swinburne.

G82 "The Theme of *Ulysses*." *Twentieth Century Studies* (November, 1969), pp. 39-40.

Repeats the assertion made in D52 that Bloom invites Stephen to go to bed with Molly: "'Greater love hath no man than this,' the epic tells us, 'that a man lay down his wife for his friend.'"

G83 Reply to Harth's comments on "Dryden's Apparent Skepticism." *Essays in Criticism* 2 (1971), pp. 111-5.

Emphasizes that Harth "stubbornly refuses even to hint at an explanation of the crucial passage (316-21)," and insists on "the noble and generous religious beliefs he had held when he was a Deist and wrote *Religio Laici*." (See D83 and I43.)

G84 "Old Men Remember with Advantages." *Arrows* (Sheffield University student magazine), No. 102 (June, 1971), pp. 8-10.

G85 Foreword to Kenneth H.C. Lo, *Peking Cookery*. London: Faber and Faber, 1971.

G86 Letter on *Mansfield Park*. *TLS* (July 14, 1972), p. 819.

G87 "Voices from the Archives." *Listener* (November 2, 1972), pp. 593-4.

A broadcast talk on the Japanese, given in 1942. (See G33.)

G88 "The Intentional Fallacy, Again." *Essays in Criticism* 23 (1972), p. 435.

Rejects the notion of the intentional fallacy, "because the students are denied any spontaneous contact with an author's mind."

G89 Letter. *TLS* (January 12, 1973), p. 40.

Responds to the highly critical review of the Coleridge volume he edited with David Pirie. (See C1 and J48.)

G90 Letter. *TLS* (May 18, 1973). p. 556.

Argues that the sonnets addressed to a patron are probably to Southampton, though poems to others may be included also (e.g., Sonnet 20). Believes it is "very probable" that Emilia Lanier was Shakespeare's Dark Lady.

G91 Letter. *TLS* (August 24, 1973), p. 978.

Disputes a textual point in Pope's "Epistle to Burlington." (See G92.)

G92 Letter. *TLS* (September 7, 1973), p. 1029.

Continues dispute over textual point started in G91. (See L1.)

G93 "The Gifts of China." *Sunday Times* (September 30, 1973).

A description of the Chinese Exhibition at the Royal Academy.

G94 Letter. *TLS* (March 8, 1974), pp. 238-9.

On Shakespeare's sonnets and on sexual innuendoes in "occupation" in Shakespeare.

G95 "Wartime Recollections." *Harvard Advocate* 108, 2-3 (1975), p. 31.

G96 William Empson, *et al*. "On Criticism." *Agenda* 14, 3 (1976), pp. 3-44.

Along with eleven other critics, gives brief answers to ten questions.

G97 "Milton's God." *PMLA* 93 (1978), p. 118.

Answers Joan Bennett's "God, Satan, and King Charles: Milton's Royal Portraits," in *PMLA* 92 (1977), pp. 441-57. Argues that the angels feel that they have won a "moral victory" in having "resisted the power of God for two days of battle." (See M3 and M4.)

G98 "Postscript." Christopher Norris, *William Empson and the Philosophy of Literary Criticism."* London: Athlone Press, 1978, pp. 205-6.

G99 Letter. *New York Review of Books* (June 1, 1978), p. 40.

Responds to a March 23, 1978, review of Christopher Hill's book on Milton, explaining that in *Milton's God* he does not present Milton as a "rude man blaspheming before a pious audience," but that he thinks Milton saw himself as "trying to answer people who were denouncing God."

G100 "William Empson Remembers I.A. Richards." *London Review of Books* (June 5-June 18, 1980), p. 14.

Comments on Richards's attempts to establish Basic English in China, and praises him for his "immense success" as a lecturer.

G101 Letter. *London Review of Books* (September 18-October 1, 1980), p. 4.

Brief note on the Tarot cards.

II. Secondary Sources

H

BOOKS AND COLLECTIONS OF ESSAYS

H1 Cianci, Giovanni. *La scuola di Cambridge: La critica letteraria di I.A. Richards, W. Empson, F.R. Leavis*. Bari, Italy, 1970.

H2 Gardner, Philip and Averill. *The God Approached. A Commentary on the Poems of William Empson*. Totowa, N.J.: Rowman and Littlefield, 1978. 226 pp.

Explicates each of Empson's collected poems, giving date and place of first publication. Excludes the four translations ("The Fool," "The Shadow," "The Small Bird to the Big," and "Chinese Ballad") and "The Birth of Steel." Includes an informative introduction, with useful notes and a bibliography. The explications are excellent--well written and suggestive--and they provide many leads to sources and analogues. Reviewed in *Encounter* 53 (July, 1979), pp. 41-8. (See K1.)

H3 Gill, Roma, ed. *William Empson: The Man and His Work*. London and Boston: Routledge and Kegan Paul, 1974. 224 pp.

Contents: 1. "A Toast," by W.H. Auden (L2); 2. "The Ambiguity of William Empson," by M.C. Bradbrook (I8); 3. "Extracts from Unpublished Memoirs," by Kathleen Raine (M41); 4. "Mr. William Empson in Japan," by Rintaro Fukuhara (I37); 5. "A Is B at 8,000 Feet," by Janet Adam Smith (M50); 6. "Empson Agonistes," by Karl Miller (I70); 7. "William Empson," by Ronald Bottrall (L5); 8. "The Man within the Name: William Empson as Poet, Critic, and Friend," by George Fraser (I32); 9. "An Eighth Type of Ambiguity," by Graham Hough (I51); 10. "Semantic Frontiersman," by I.A. Richards (I83); 11. "All or Nothing: A Theme in John Donne," by L.C. Knights; 12. "Reflections on Johnson's *Life of Milton*," by John Wain; 13. "*New Signatures* in Retrospect," by A.G. Stock (I93); 14. "Empson's Poetry," by Christopher Ricks (I84); 15. "William Empson," by Francis Berry (L4); 16. "An Empson Bibliography," by Moira Megaw (M26).

A *Festschrift*, for which the contributors were asked to write about "the man himself, or his works, or the subjects that interested him." Reviewed in *TLS* (June 7, 1974), pp. 597-8 (see K4); *Encounter* 43 (November, 1974), pp. 75-9 (see K5); *Critical Quarterly* 18 (1976), pp. 90-6 (see K6); *Eigo Seinen* (Tokyo) 120 (1974), pp. 356-8; *Sewanee Review* 83 (1975), pp. xlvi-li (see K8); *New York Review of Books* (January 23, 1975), pp. 30-3 (see K9).

H4 Meller, Horst. *Das Gedicht als Einübung: Zum Dichtungsverständnis William Empsons*. Heidelberg: Carl Winter-Universitätsverlag, 1974. 244 pp.

Contents:

II DER POET ALS SEMANTIKER: William Empsons Dichtungsbetrachtung im Arbeitsklima seiner Kontextsemantik
- 9 Mikroskopie des poetischen Kontexts: *Seven Types of Ambiguity*
- 10 William Empsons Standort zwischen I.A. Richards und T.S. Eliot
- 11 Gesellschaftliche Dimensionen des Kontext-Theorems: *Some Versions of Pastoral* und *The Structure of Complex Words*

III DIE LITERARISCHE SZENE ALS MORALISCHES TRIBUNAL: Zum Kontext von *Milton's God*
- 12 Verräterische Dissonanzen im Milton's "Pastorale der Unschuld von Mensch und Natur"
- 13 Die literarische Tonart der Anklageschrift
- 14 Empson und die neo-christlichen Wege zum *Verlorenen Paradies*
- 15 Kampfansage an den Titelhelden--und die agnostische Alternative

IV DAS GEDICHT ALS GERONNENES DENKSPIEL: Paradigmen der Einübung in William Empsons Lyrik
- 16 Auf der Suche nach poetischer Identität: *Rolling the Lawn*
- 17 Politische Tagessatire als Pastiche und Puzzlespiel des *wit*: *Part of Mandevil's Travels*
- 18 Warnung vor den Fallstricken der Philosophen: *Dissatisfaction with Metaphysics*
- 19 Metaphysische Liebeslyrik im Denkraum neuester *New Philosophy*: Zum *Arachne*-Gedicht
- 20 Ein Stil aus einer Verzweiflung: *This Last Pain*

Reviewed in *Germanisch-romanische Monatsschrift* (Heidelberg), 28 (1978), pp. 254-7.

H5 Morelli, Angelo. *La Poesia di William Empson*. Catania, Italy: Giannotta, 1959. 154 pp.

H6 Norris, Christopher. *William Empson and the Philosophy of Literary Criticism*. London: Athlone Press, 1978. 222 pp.

Contents:

Reviewed in *New Statesman* 96 (August 11, 1978), pp. 185-6 (see K11); *Virginia Quarterly Review* 55 (Summer, 1979), pp. 540-5 (see K12); *Encounter* 53 (July, 1979), pp. 41-8 (see K1).

A published version of M2.

Chapter 1. Explains how the New Critics found much in Empson's work to use but judged him heretical on key issues. Since returning from Asia in 1951 Empson has worked steadily against the formalists and the Neo-Christians. He has fought for the continuity of prose and a rational poetry that "argufies," rejecting Symbolist doctrines and keeping poetry open to and available for public debate. His theory of language "undermines the assumptions of behaviourism and lays the ground for a rationalist philosophy of mind." Norris is excellent in explaining the relationship of the practical chapters in *Complex Words* to the "conceptual machinery": "The theory is more a background of assurance, a generalised set of assumptions, than a rigid logical frame on which to hang the late chapters."

Speculates that Empson's later poems--after 1935--are less concentrated because of his preoccupation with *Complex Words*: his distrust of the emotive would not have been congenial to the writing of poetry. Between *Seven Types* and *Complex Words* Empson moves from verbal analysis (which points toward formalism) to "the wider human background of knowledge and experience." In Empson, the dangers of "reading in" meanings and the scepticism of anti-intentionalists are swept aside by his conviction that knowledge and sympathy can triumph in adequate understanding, and for Norris any resulting "ethical colouring" is no more pronounced than the "proto-theological bias" found in the readings of the New Critics.

Analyzes Empson's quarrels with critics like Hugh Kenner, stressing that Empson's approach to criticism "declares literature an open field for moral interpretation" and "allows the interpreter a certain licence of self-expression." Points out that despite his stance against the Symbolists and the Neo-Christians, Empson has repeatedly studied works in these traditions.

Chapter 2. Distinguishes Empson from the American formalists and the Cambridge critics of the 1930's, showing how he avoided "threatening regularities" and refused to "erect his readings into abstract principle." Stresses the rational humanism of Empson's criticism: "He pursues the implications of poetry, not into their formal extension as properties of poetic structure, but into the human context of a rich and diverse experience to which--on his principled assumption--they ultimately appeal."

Explains Pastoral as Empson's means of expressing his sense of progress in history, a view of man and society opposed to "the timeless, disengaged aesthetic of literary Symbolism." "Pastoral may be seen, then, as a cover-term for the whole questioning process of moving 'beyond formalism' to reinstate somehow the various 'heresies'-- the subjective element--proscribed by the New Critics." Argues that "Pastoral provided a root metaphor, a 'subjective correlative,' for the complicated feelings which demanded expression in Empson's early writing."

Chapter 3. Traces the "inexplicit content of theory" in Empson's criticism, finding it to be "internally generated" by the "practical encounter of critic with text." Empson's theory has parallels with drama in that his interpretations "rest always on the complex interchange of feelings found most typically in a responsive theatre audience." Empson values the idea of "generalisation," which capitalizes on the "background" behind great poetry and "becomes the logic of poetic language and the source of any possible validation of critical judgement." *Complex Words* reveals a more sophisticated understanding of intention than did *Seven Types*; in *Complex Words* "Meanings are articulate, accountable in terms of an ordered 'grammar', and above all an evidence of 'motivation'." Identifies self-interest as the "one reliable basis for mutual understanding" advanced by Empson.

Ascribes to Empson in *Complex Words* an eighteenth-century commonsense ethic that rejects "tragic" values and embraces "a trust in human nature based on a shared knowledge of its needs and attendant weaknesses." *Complex Words* "interprets meanings which have somehow freed themselves from the high religious sanctions, or 'official' morality, of Christian tradition." The political background to this view is developed in *Some Versions of Pastoral*, where the collapse of the king's divine right leads in Pastoral to the replacement of the hero with "his inverted likeness, the rogue."

Chapter 4. Places Empson's ideas on language and meaning in a context of modern linguistic philosophy, clarifying how Empson avoids identifying meaning with the emotive and the contextual. Grammar is both normative and descriptive for Empson, and a word carries its own "structure of intelligible usage" independent of context and charged with authorial intention. Intuïtion, which has its affinities with Symbolism, has no place in Empson's vision of a community of readers made possible by a shared use of commonsense reasoning; and Brooks's approach through the "hermeneutic rules of an orthodox rhetoric" is equally antagonistic to Empson's philosophy. Norris notes Empson's resistance to any "picture-theory" of the relationship between thought and language: "No kind of visualized logical projection, whatsoever its subtleties of form, can attain to the richness of felt implication which occupies the critic and (properly) the philosopher of language."

Stresses the Augustan aspect of *Complex Words*, the "hard-put rationalism and commonsense ethic," and asserts a "set of moral premises" implicit in Empson's explorations of rich words like 'fool.' Elucidates Empson's opposition to semanticists like C.S. Lewis and Leo Spitzer, whose "theocentric" orientation toward language study leads them to posit God-given etymons that Empson rejects in favor of usages that "depend very largely on the intentional acts, the sensitive verbal resources of individual speakers and writers." Identifies Empson as a humanist whose "renaissance" view of the freedom available in language contrasts with Spitzer's yearning for the "medieval harmonies of faith and received wisdom," citing as evidence Empson's disagreements with Rosemond Tuve (see M61, D40, F78), J. Dover Wilson (see D43, D47), and Maynard Mack (see D76).

In an appendix to this chapter, Norris finds formal support for Empson's "logico-linguistic arguments" in Jerrold J. Katz's *Semantic Theory*, concluding that in practice Empson "achieves something like the distinction which Katz maintains between formalised logic and semantic open-endedness."

Chapter 5. Identifies the critics most influenced by Empson as those who found his techniques of verbal analysis "a useful adjunct to theology"; pairs off Empson and Husserl against Eliot and Bradley as proponents of, respectively, "subjective" and "objective" theories of perception and intention. Links *Milton's God* to Empson's earlier works by the attempt in it "to mark off the *intentional* character of poetry from the regions of myth and paradox." Explains Empson's rejection of Imagism as part of his emphasis on the rational powers of poetry. Depicts the uneasiness with which Empson appoaches "paradox, metaphysics, and themes of the 'deep' subconscious," finding that *Some Versions of Pastoral* assumes no clear division in creativity between the conscious and the unconscious. Remarks on the "alliance" Empson finds between the Neo-Christians and the Symbolists, including the support they derive from the Unconscious, and describes the way Empson has deflected critical attention from the Unconscious to social values. Identifies the particular value of plot to Empson's approach: where plot can be found, rational explanations are also possible. Finds "problems of credibility" in Empson's work on Donne, Milton, and Coleridge, where the anti-Christian motive is so strong.

Chapter 6. Points to the source of Empson's humanism in Benthamism. Contrasts Empson's approval of a "two-way questioning exchange" with the "largely self-validating" criticism of Leavis and Eliot. Empson's humanism "largely revalues the tragic morality of self-surrender and renunciation," and his critical methods "represent an active and continuing moral debate." Judges Empson pre-eminent in his coming to grips with the significance of modern rationalism for criticism. Weighs the importance to Empson of Eastern ethical systems, finding them also limited by his rationalism: "Empson's experience of Far-Eastern cultures made the business of rational explanation seem all the more urgent and general a problem." Stresses Empson's avoidance of "specialized theoretical activity" and the "central idea of Empson's criticism, that one ought to accept any likely 'theory', however remote or problematic, which throws some light on an author's practical intentions."

H7 *The Review: A Magazine of Poetry and Criticism* (June, 1963).

A special issue devoted to Empson. Reviewed in *Essays in Criticism* 14 (1964), pp. 91-101 (see K13).

Contents:

Martin Dodsworth. "Empson at Cambridge," p. 3. (See I18.)

Philip Hobsbaum. "Empson As Critical Practitioner," p. 14. (See I47.)

John Fuller. "Empson's Tone," p. 21. (See I38.)

William Empson. "In Conversation with Christopher Ricks," p. 26. (See I84.)

Ian Hamilton. "A Girl Can't Go On Laughing All the Time," p. 36. (See I41.)

Saul Touster. "Empson's Legal Fiction," p. 45. (See I99.)

Colin Falck. "This Deep Blankness," p. 49. (See I26.)

Peter Lowbridge. "An Empson Bibliography," p. 63. (See M25.)

L.E. Sissman. "Just a Whack at Empson," p. 75. (See L31.)

H8 Sale, Roger. "The Achievement of William Empson." In *Modern Heroism*. Berkeley, Los Angeles, London: University of California Press, 1973. Pp. 107-92.

Highly appreciative essay, concentrating on *Seven Types* and *Some Versions of Pastoral*, arguing for Empson as a "hero who seeks to create with his readers a community such as those created earlier in the culture by pastoral literature." Stresses the influence on Empson of Eliot's idea of history being continually created by the writer and of the need to see the present in relation to the past; but points out that whereas Eliot keeps writers at a distance, Empson's need for community impels him to criticism that brings past and present together. Attributes a genuine unified sensibility to Empson, who, as a historian of pastoral, defies the Myth of Lost Unity with his own personal code. Discovers that *Seven Types*, beneath the froth of talk about ambiguity, works subtly to subvert nineteenth-century commonplaces and reveals Empson as one of the "great literary moralists." Admits that *Some Versions of Pastoral* is "hard going" but maintains it develops a coherent subject: "the collapse of the old pastoral relation of the swain-hero to the sheep-people and the consequences of that collapse in the period between the end of the sixteenth and the end of the nineteenth century." Discerns a "considerable retreat" in *Complex Words* from the earlier striving for community and an unpleasant dogmatism in most of the later works: "he was much more persuasive when he was not trying to preach at all."

Reviewed in *TLS* (July 27, 1973), p. 848 (see K14); *Modern Language Quarterly* 35 (1974), pp. 92-5 (see K15); *New York Review of Books* (January 24, 1974), pp. 43-6 (see K16); *Modern Philology* 73 (1975), pp. 100-104 (see K17); *Modern Fiction Studies* 19 (1973), pp. 636-8 (see K18).

H9 Willis, J.H.,Jr. *William Empson*. No. 39 in "Columbia Essays on Modern Writers." New York and London: Columbia University Press, 1969.

Brief, well written overview of Empson's career, praising the "obvious strength, sanity, and balance of his mind."

I

ESSAYS AND REVIEW ARTICLES

I1 Adams, Robert Martin. "Empson and Bentley: Something about Milton Too." *Partisan Review* 21 (March-April, 1954), pp. 178-89.

Spells out in detail Empson's misquotations and faulty attributions in his Bentley essay in *Some Versions of Pastoral*. Asserts that epics like *Paradise Lost* should not fairly be subjected to close analyses of their imagery. A severely dismissive essay.

I1a Adams, Robert Martin. "Empson and Bentley: Scherzo." In *Ikon: John Milton and the Modern Critics*. Ithaca: Cornell University Press, 1955. Pp. 112-27. (Reprinted in 1966 as *Milton and the Modern Critics*.)

Reprint of I1.

I2 Alpers, Paul. "Empson on Pastoral." *New Literary History* 10 (1978), pp. 101-23.

Calls *Some Versions of Pastoral* "brilliant" but difficult to use, and identifies the "two main ideas that run through it: first, that 'the pastoral process' consists of 'putting the complex into the simple,' and second, that pastoral has a unifying social force, and is a means of bridging differences and reconciling social classes." Explains the oblique approach in *Some Versions of Pastoral* as Empson's "way of dealing with the central puzzles of freedom and determinism." Stresses the incompleteness for Empson of critical analysis--"simply a human aid like any other"--and emphasizes the importance of social convention for Empson. Analyzes Empson's aversion to tragic and metaphysical visions: "The human condition, to him, is always historical and social, and on the highest throne in the world we are still sitting only on our own rump."

One of the best discussions of Empson's criticism.

I3 Alvarez, Alfred. "William Empson: A Style from a Despair." In *Stewards of Excellence: Studies in Modern English and American Poets*. New York: Charles Scribner's Sons, 1958. Pp. 73-86.

Asserts that Empson's intellectual poems became popular around 1950 as a relief from the incoherent poetry of the war. The early poems reflect a sharp sensitivity to the ideas of their time: the "sceptical, semi-scientific tough-mindedness of Cambridge in the late twenties." The poems have an "*essential* objectivity" in that the early difficult poetry "of the conceit" turns personal energy into a "particularly impersonal business"; and in the later poems "personal feeling comes out as something more general." Devoted to wit and a clever performance, Empson is more like the minor Metaphysicals than like Donne.

I4 Bateson, F.W. "The Function of Criticism at the Present Time." *Essays in Criticism* 3 (1953), pp. 1-27.

Includes a discussion (pp. 7-9) of Empson's commentary on "bare ruined choirs" in *Seven Types*, calling it a "characteristic specimen of Empsonian irresponsibility." (See G36 and I5.)

I5 Bateson, F.W. Answer to G36. *Essays in Criticism* 3 (1953), pp. 358-62.

Continues his dialogue with Empson on "bare ruined choirs," dismissing Empson's allusion to monastic choirs as "historically improbable" and "poetically disastrous." (See L4.)

I6 Blackburn, Thomas. *The Price of an Eye*. New York: William Morrow, 1961.

Admiring comment (pp. 141-2) on "This Last Pain" and "Missing Dates." "But the unraveling of much of his verse may depend on an interest in crossword puzzles rather than poetry."

I7 Borklund, Elmer. "Empson, William." In *Contemporary Literary Critics*. New York: St. Martin's Press; London: St. James Press, 1977. Pp. 180-7.

Concise, well written, balanced summaries and judgments of the four books of criticism. Includes selected primary and secondary bibliographies, plus a paragraph of biographical data. A useful reference.

I8 Bradbrook, M.C. "The Ambiguity of William Empson." In *William Empson: The Man and His Work*, ed. Roma Gill. London and Boston: Routledge and Kegan Paul, 1974. Pp. 2-12.

Finds Empson's "mathematically agile" analyses to be "rooted in a much warmer and richer organic response to complex human situations embodied in Nature," part of which is a Coleridgean balancing of opposites. When he wrote *Seven Types*, Empson was "close to his work as a mathematician," and Eliot's praise of the scientific mind exhibiting "general intelligence" "offers a definition of Empson's criticism at its best." Thus Bradbrook concludes of Empson's criticism that "His unity of close concentration and wide-ranging perspectives is perhaps the most applied form of applied mathematics that the university of Bertrand Russell has ever turned out."

I9 Breitkreuz, Hartmut. "Empson's 'The Beautiful Train.'" *Explicator* 31 (1972), Item 9.

I9a Breikreuz, Hartmut. "William Empsons 'The Beautiful Train.'" *Archiv* 209 (1972), pp. 119-22.

I9 in German.

I10 Brooks, Cleanth. "Empson's Criticism." In *"Accent" Anthology: Selections from "Accent," A Quarterly of New Literature, 1940-1945*, ed. Kerker Quinn and Charles Shattuck. New York: Harcourt, Brace and Company, 1946. Pp. 496-508.

Stimulating defense of Empson and of the analysis of multiple meanings. The significance of *Seven Types*, "which reads for the most part like uncommonly good talk," is that it deals with "what the poem 'means' in terms of its structure *as a poem*." Empson is not like past critics who "attempted to find the goodness of the poem ... in terms of its prose argument ... or in the charm of the decorative elements." Metaphor and metrics become functional. The framework of *Seven Types* may be defective, but the defect does not matter for "the brilliant asides" and the "analytical commentaries" are "the important thing." As for the slips, "the slips are just that," and of the critics who charge that Empson's readings are idiosyncratic, "one need only ask to be allowed to examine the proof."

An excellent essay, worth comparing with the position taken by Raines in *Defending Ancient Springs*. (See I79.)

I11 Brooks, Cleanth. "Gray's Storied Urn." In *The Well Wrought Urn: Studies in the Structure of Poetry*. New York: Reynal and Hitchcock, 1947. Pp. 96-113.

Referring to Empson's discussion of Gray's "Churchyard" ode: "Empson, in his anxiety to establish the 'latent political ideas,' has extended the implications a little further than the total context of the whole poem warrants." (See D12b.)

I11a Brooks, Cleanth. "Gray's Storied Urn." In *The Well Wrought Urn: Studies in the Structure of Poetry*. New York: Harcourt, Brace & World, n.d. Pp. 105-23.

Paperback reprint of I11.

I12 Brooks, Cleanth, and William K. Wimsatt, Jr. *Literary Criticism: A Short History*. New York: Alfred A. Knopf, 1957. Pp. 635-56.

Includes discussion of Empson in a chapter on "The Semantic Principle," stressing his "general psychologistic bias" and citing his "substantial achievement" in semantic analysis. Observes that Empson's curiosity leads sometimes to a "search for puzzles." Except for a brief reference to the cognitive position forwarded in *Complex Words*, the discussion is limited to *Seven Types*.

I13 Burgum, Edwin Berry. "The Cult of the Complex in Poetry." *Science and Society* 15 (Winter, 1951), pp. 31-48.

Part I attacks Empson, whose *Seven Types* "almost begins a new era in the criticism of poetry," and whose method "ignores the social or historical referent." Argues that Empson's ambiguity--a term for what has been traditionally known as metaphor--predisposes him to favor "the poetry of the casuist." Most seriously, "his method sets up a tendency to regard the value of a poem as proportional to the quantity of ambiguity in it," thereby resulting in a dismissal of a great deal of poetry on no other grounds.

I14 Chapman, Raymond. "Words and Meanings." In *Linguistics and Literature: An Introduction to Literary Stylistics*. London: Edward Arnold, 1973. Pp. 58-71.

Identifies Empson as the source of modern attitudes toward ambiguity, and notes that "in linguistics *ambiguity* is usually taken with reference to the problem of sentences which seem identical in surface structure but have different deep meanings."

I15 Combecher, Hans. "William Empson: Legal Fiction." *Deutung englischer Gedichte*. Heft 1 (Frankfurt, 1965), pp. 111-4.

I16 Danby, John. "William Empson." *Critical Quarterly* 1 (Summer, 1959), pp. 99-104.

Speculates on the reasons why both the matter and the manner of Empson's poems were more successful in the fifties than in the thirties. Generally hostile.

I17 Das, B. "A Note on the Poetry of William Empson." *Literary Criterion* (Mysore) 6 (1965), pp. 11-18.

I18 Dodsworth, Martin. "Empson at Cambridge." *The Review: A Magazine of Poetry and Criticism*. (June, 1963), pp. 3-13.

Sketches Empson's activities at Cambridge and

discusses several early poems, concluding that "Empson succeeded in subordinating his natural zest and energy to facing problems most of us would rather not face."

I19 Donoghue, Denis. *Ferocious Alphabets.* Boston and Toronto: Little, Brown and Company, 1981. Pp. 71-7.

Discusses Empson in a chapter on "Style As Compensation." Style compensates for "defects in the conditions of writing," such as the writer's insecurities about his readers. In the Cambridge writers Richards, Leavis, and Empson, the style emerges as "worried pretense" and reveals a writer "desperate" to assuage human loneliness by improving communication and creating a community." Empson's poetry and essays are both invitations to a dialogue, written with a fear that no one is listening. Empson, Richards, and Leavis are propagandists against loneliness, not seduced by the notion of the world as language, and as content with one set of words as another. Notes in a separate discussion (p. 29) that "Imperialism is never far from Empson's own style, which has a way of dividing people into English and Others." Also includes Empson with several other English scholars who practice "gunboat linguistics": "They seem to claim, by their style rather than overtly, that they represent what Arnold called 'the tone of the center,' which casts other people as provincial."

I20 Donoghue, Denis. "Reading a Poem: Empson's 'Arachne.'" *Studies* 45 (Summer, 1956), pp. 219-26.

Lists the first-rate Empson poems: "Arachne," "Legal Fiction," "Missing Dates," "Letter II," "To an Old Lady," "This Last Pain," and "Manchouli." Describes Empson as a didactic poet, "heir to Pope rather than to Donne," but "born into an age in which no positive values are shared." Emphasizes that "Arachne" is "a love-poem throughout" and praises the "tremendously complex attitude to man" implicit in the king spider image.

I21 Drew, Elizabeth. *Poetry: A Modern Guide to Its Understanding and Enjoyment.* New York: W.W. Norton, 1959. Pp. 138-40.

Discusses Empson's poem "Missing Dates," praising its refrains but concluding that "it comes through strongly only in the last four lines where the metaphysical ingenuities are dropped."

I22 Drew, Elizabeth, and John Sweeney. *Directions in Modern Poetry.* New York: W.W. Norton, 1940. Pp. 81-3 and 204-7.

Brief discussions of "Note on Local Flora" and "Legal Fiction," stressing their "intense compression and mental subtlety."

I23 Duncan, Joseph. "William Empson." In *The Revival of Metaphysical Poetry: The History of a Style, 1800 to the Present.* New York: Octagon Books, 1969. Pp. 196-202.

Compares Empson's poetry to Donne's, judging Empson to be more "cerebral" and finding that he captures the appeal of Planck and Einstein's new physics, as well as that of the popular crossword puzzle. Empson has an "analogizing" mind and his figures depend less on systems of thoughts than Donne's do. Empson is more self-consciously intellectual than Donne--"but perhaps he is most himself when he is something of a showoff."

I24 Durrell, Lawrence. *A Key to Modern Poetry.* London: Peter Nevill; Norman: University of Oklahoma, 1952. Pp. 198-9.

Praises Empson the poet for the way "he has disturbed syntax to force multiple meanings upon the structure of words."

I25 Eberhart, Richard. "Empson's Poetry." In *"Accent" Anthology: Selections from "Accent," A Quarterly of New Literature, 1940-1945*, ed. Kerker Quinn and Charles Shattuck. New York: Harcourt, Brace and Company, 1946. Pp. 571-88.

An enthusiastic appreciation by a poet who was "up at Cambridge coterminously with Empson," including a commentary on "This Last Pain." The glimpses of the Cambridge milieu and of the impact of Empson's poetry ("It was all so intellectual, so very exciting, so very Cantabridgean") should be compared with the reminiscence by Raine. (See M42.)

I26 Falck, Colin. "This Deep Blankness." *The Review: A Magazine of Poetry and Criticism.* (June, 1963), pp. 49-62.

Outlines the opposition in modern philosophy between discourse and imagery, finding that "our best modern poetics has in fact been a series of attempts to rationalise and domesticate the Romantic-Symbolist tradition." Admires the "driving assurance of the metaphysical style" in Empson's best poems, but charges that they demand "a general obliviousness to the connotations of things which is quite remote from the modern sensibility." Concludes, then, that "what Empson has done is in its own way heroic; it is a kind of Götterdämmerung of the rationalist intellect, and it is unrepeatable."

I27 Fish, Stanley. "Literature in the Reader: Affective Stylistics." *New Literary History* 2 (1970), pp. 123-62.

In an essay that tries to "substitute the structure of the reader's experience for the formal structures of the text," Fish finds that "Empson does not follow the form of the reader's experience, but some form, usually arbitrary, which allows him to explore in depth isolated moments or potential moments in that experience."

I27a Fish, Stanley. "Literature in the Reader: Affective Stylistics." Appendix to *Self-Consuming Artifacts: The Experience of Seventeenth-Century Literature.* Berkeley and London: University of California Press, 1972. Pp. 383-427.

Reprint of I27.

I27b Fish, Stanley. "Literature in the Reader: Affective Stylistics." In *Is There a Text in This Class? The Authority of Interpretive Communities*. Cambridge, Mass. and London, Harvard University Press, 1980. Pp. 21-67.

Reprint of I27.

I28 Fish, Stanley. "The Harassed Reader in *Paradise Lost*." *Critical Quarterly* 7 (Summer, 1965), pp. 162-82.

Expanded in I28b. See I28b for annotation.

I28a Fish, Stanley. "The Harassed Reader in *Paradise Lost*." In *Milton, "Paradise Lost": A Casebook*, ed. A.E. Dyson and Julian Lovelock. London: Macmillan, 1973. Pp. 152-78.

Reprint of I28. Also see "Introduction," pp. 11-24, for comments on Empson and Fish.

I28b Fish, Stanley. *Surprised by Sin: The Reader in "Paradise Lost."* London: Macmillan; New York: St. Martin's Press, 1967.

Only infrequent references to Empson, but there is a feeling that Empson is not far from Fish's mind as he develops his central point: "Milton's method is to re-create in the mind of the reader ... the drama of the Fall, to make him fall again exactly as Adam did...." Challenges Empson directly at one place: "If Empson's law--'all the characters are on trial in any civilized narrative'--applies at all to Milton's God, its application is rhetorical."

I29 Ford, Newell F. "Empson's and Ransom's Mutilations of Texts." *Philological Quarterly* 29 (1950), pp. 81-4.

Totals up Empson's misquotations in *Seven Types* of Keats, Shelley, and Wordsworth.

I30 Forrest-Thomson, Veronica. "Rational Artifice: Some Remarks on the Poetry of William Empson." *Yearbook of English Studies* 4 (1974), pp. 225-38.

Argues, partly from a close reading of "High Dive," "that Empson's conscious assumption of a style that was 'artificial' and 'anachronistic' according to the assumptions of his period implied a specially valued awareness that such a style was the only possible way to maintain the function of the poet, his contact with his literary past and with his ideological present."

I31 Fowler, Roger, and Peter Mercer. "Criticism and the Language of Literature." *Style* 3 (1969), pp. 45-72.

Pages 55-58 are devoted to the importance of *Seven Types,* which remains "the major, and continuing, stimulus to descriptive criticism in England."

I32 Fraser, George. "The Man within the Name: William Empson as Poet, Critic, and Friend." In *William Empson: The Man and His Work*, ed. Roma Gill. London and Boston: Routledge and Kegan Paul, 1974. Pp. 52-75.

Believes that among those who know him Empson is thought of primarily as a poet. Sketches the sudden fame and influence gained by *Seven Types*, pointing out that Empson's most productive period as a poet came while he was writing *Seven Types* and *Some Versions of Pastoral*. Praises the rhythms of Empson's poems and suggests that Saussure's distinction between *le signifiant* and *le signifie* might be applied fruitfully to the poems. Repeats Richards's judgment that *Complex Words* is "too much of a palimpsest," but appreciates the "splendid vigour" of *Milton's God* even though "Milton is a bad stick to beat Christianity with."

I33 Fraser, G.S. *The Modern Writer and His World.* New York: Criterion, 1955. Pp. 256-61.

Stresses the scientific background Empson enjoys ("perhaps the most bewildering of modern poets"), but points out that "these intellectual complexities are balanced and corrected by an admirable simplicity of human approach." Sums up Empson's "notion" of the pastoral mode: that writing which "evades the current issues of life in a complex society by inventing, or at least depicting with a certain added glow of poetic tenderness, a world of simple characters and simpler pleasures than those of the actual world."

I34 Fraser, G.S. "'Not Wrongly Moved ...' (William Empson)." In *Vision and Rhetoric: Studies in Modern Poetry*. New York: Barnes and Noble, Inc., 1960. Pp. 193-201.

Observations on the "art and temperament and moral attitudes" in Empson's poems. The "moral framework" that informs Empson's poems comprises "a religious temperament, a scientific world view, the attitude to politics of a traditional English liberal of the best kind, a constitutional melancholy and a robust good-humour, a sardonic wit, a gift for expressing the diffidence and passion of romantic personal attachments, a belief in pleasure, a scepticism about abstract systems, and a sharply practical impatience with anything he considers cant."

I34a "'Not Wrongly Moved ...' (William Empson). *Essays on Twentieth-Century Poets*. Totowa, New Jersey: Rowman and Littlefield, 1977. Pp. 162-8.

Reprint of I34.

I35 Fraser, G.S. "On the Interpretation of the Difficult Poem." In *Interpretations: Essays on Twelve English Poems*, ed. John Wain. London: Routledge and Kegan Paul, 1955. Pp. 211-37.

Gives a detailed Freudian analysis of Empson's "The Teasers," judging its broader subject to be "an argument about thought and feeling." Insists that the poem makes complete sense only when understood as "a statement by a man like Empson, in his time and place." John Wain says of "The Teasers" in his introduction to this volume that its argument is "not even broadly establishable"

(p. xii), and Fraser's discussion is cast largely in the form of a response to Wain's essay "Ambiguous Gifts: Notes on the Poetry of William Empson." (See I101.)

I36 Fraser, G.S. "William Empson." In *Contemporary Poets*, 3rd edition, ed. James Vinson. New York: St. Martin's Press, 1980. Pp. 437-9.

Empson's poems "do not lend themselves to simple summary in terms of theme," but leave "a peculiar flavour, tart, fibrous, captivating, like that of a quince or crab apple." Empson responds that "I cannot really feel pleased when he tells you at the end not to bother about the arguments. They are what the poetry is made out of, whether the result is good or bad."

I37 Fukuhara, Rintaro. "Mr. William Empson in Japan." In *William Empson: The Man and His Work*, ed. Roma Gill. London and Boston: Routledge and Kegan Paul, 1974. Pp. 21-33.

Recollections of Empson by the man who was his department head in Japan.

I38 Fuller, John. "Empson's Tone." *The Review: A Magazine of Poetry and Criticism*. (June, 1963), pp. 21-5.

Locates the source of Empson's tone in his formal struggles with his "brilliance of detail."

I39 Gardner, Philip. "'Meaning' in the Poetry of William Empson." *Humanities Association Bulletin* (Canada) 18 (Spring, 1967), pp. 75-86.

Surveys the critical response to Empson's poetry; explicates "Part of Mandevil's Travels"; identifies four sources of difficulty in understanding Empson's poems: verbal ambiguities, compression, mathematical and scientific allusions, other allusions. Pleads for making an honest attempt at understanding the poems before judging Empson.

I40 Glicksberg, Charles I. "William Empson: Genius of Ambiguity." *Dalhousie Review* 29 (1950), pp. 366-77.

Applauds Empson's rational analyses of poetry but condemns what he considers the excesses committed: "For those who are interested primarily in poetry and only secondarily in the virtuosity of the critic, Empson's work and that of his followers must be rejected as misleading, sometimes dangerously so."

I41 Hamilton, Ian. "A Girl Can't Go On Laughing All the Time." *The Review: A Magazine of Poetry and Criticism*. (June, 1963), pp. 36-44.

States his case plainly: "No amount of misleading talk about Donne can escape the fact that the bulk of Empson's early verse is unattractively obscure...." Denies that Empson has made a scientific vocabulary available in his poems. The later "political" poems are marred by his being "somewhat too anxious to take an original stand" and "an uneasy wavering between the didactic and the whimsical...."

I41a Hamilton, Ian. "William Empson." In *A Poetry Chronicle*. London: Faber and Faber, 1973. Pp. 37-44.

Reprint of I41.

I42 Hardy, Barbara. "The Critics Who Made Us--William Empson and *Seven Types of Ambiguity*." *Sewanee Review* 90 (Summer, 1982), pp. 430-9.

A recollection of what *Seven Types* meant to the author when she was an undergraduate at University College, London, in the 1940's: "this sophisticated criticism was written out of a full experience, and though that experience didn't find a place in the analysis, its existence was unobtrusively and easily implicit in the humor, in the personal tone, in the paraphrases or translations into racy modern English."

I43 Harth, Phillip. "Empson's Interpretation of *Religio Laici*." *Essays in Criticism* 20 (1970), pp. 446-50.

Rejects Empson's claim of covert deist sympathies in Dryden's *Religio Laici*, ll. 311-21, finding a Christian argument in the lines. (See D83 and G83.)

I44 Hartman, Geoffrey. "Toward Literary History." *Daedalus* 99 (Spring, 1970), pp. 355-83.

Surveys modern theories of literary form, interpreting I.A. Richards as advancing a functional concept of form that stresses its unifying, reconciling, civilizing virtues. Empson is then declared as having "tried to escape it by postulating 'types' of ambiguity which showed how precarious this unity was, or how rebellious language."

I44a Hartman, Geoffrey. "Toward Literary History." In *In Search of Literary Theory*, ed. Morton Bloomfield. Ithaca and London: Cornell University Press, 1972. Pp. 195-235.

Reprint of I44.

I45 Hawthorne, J.M. "Commitment in the Poetry of William Empson." *Trivium* 4 (1969), pp. 21-30.

Rejects the judgments of those who find the "crossword-puzzle" element dominant in Empson's poetry, concluding that "unless the ultimately moral basis of his poetry is accepted, it had better not be read at all."

I46 Hedges, William. "The Empson Treatment." *Accent* 17 (Winter, 1957), pp. 231-41.

Explores in great detail Empson's poem "Four Legs, Three Legs, Two Legs."

I47 Hobsbaum, Philip. "Empson As Critical Practitioner." *The Review: A Magazine of Poetry and Criticism*. (June, 1963), pp. 14-20.

Finds Empson to be a practical critic, who, as "a purveyor himself of Grecian urns," approaches a poem "from the inside." Empson's biggest weakness is that, "at times, his sympathy outruns his judgement." Compared to a great scholar-critic like Leavis, Empson is unsystematic; but his readings of the classics show them to be still alive, and he will remain a favorite of the "erratic and irreverent creative artist."

I48 Hobsbaum, Philip. *Theory of Criticism*. Bloomington and London: Indiana University Press, 1970.

Summarizes (pp. 131-41) the modern readings of Herbert's "The Sacrifice," concluding of Tuve and Empson that "there is surprisingly little divergence in their views of the poem." (See D40 and M62a, as well as Chapter 7 in A1.)

I49 Hoshino, Toru. "Tairitsu to Soho--Empson no Hihyo no Gainen-sochi." *Eigo Seinen* (Tokyo) 119 (1973), pp. 146-7.

Translates as "Opposite and Complementary--Notions of Empson's Criticism."

I50 Hotopf, W.H.N. *Language, Thought, and Comprehension: A Case Study of the Writings of I.A. Richards*. London: Routledge and Kegan Paul, 1965. 349 pp.

Chapter VII of this excellent study of Richards's thought is devoted to an analysis of the understanding--and misunderstanding--of Richards's ideas by Empson (pp. 169-76) and the American New Critics. Contends that Empson, whose "eye is like that of an insect, thousand-faceted," often misunderstood Richards quite badly. Empson's "concern for the *particular*" clashed with Richards's way of thinking "in terms of very general categories." For example, Empson described Richards's idea of pseudo-statements as "inspiring lies told by the poets" (*Complex Words*, p. 426), but Richards was "totally opposed to the use of lies in poetry" and meant his remarks "as a warning that the function of poetry is not the providing of information."

I51 Hough, Graham. "An Eighth Type of Ambiguity." In *William Empson: The Man and His Work*, ed. Roma Gill. London and Boston: Routledge and Kegan Paul, 1974. Pp. 76-97.

Credits Empson with setting off the search for "multiple and simultaneous meaning" in poetry. Sketches the issues in the modern controversy over intention, explaining Austin's doctrine of illocutionary acts and concluding that "to identify the illocutionary act performed by a text or part of a text is sometimes impossible, sometimes possible, desirable where possible, but always insufficient as an interpretation of the text." Proposes that behind Empson's seven types of ambiguity "there lurks an eighth--ambiguity between intended and achieved meaning." Illustrates his thesis with the example of *Paradise Lost*, in which Milton is consciously creating a "Renaissance syncretist epic" but with unintended consequences--"that the society in hell seems so much better than that in heaven." "Neither 'the words on the page' nor 'the intentions of the author' can alone reveal the significance of a work of literature, and no adequate interpretation of a poem has ever been made by the exclusive pursuit of either of these phantoms."

I51a Hough, Graham. "An Eighth Type of Ambiguity." In *On Literary Intention*, ed. David Newton-de Molina. Edinburgh: Edinburgh University Press, 1976. Pp. 222-41.

Reprint of I51.

I51b Hough, Graham. "An Eighth Type of Ambiguity." *Selected Essays*. London and New York: Cambridge University Press, 1978. Pp. 23-45.

Reprint of I51.

I52 Hough, Graham. *Style and Stylistics*. London: Routledge and Kegan Paul; New York: Humanities Press, 1969. Pp. 90-5.

Describes *Seven Types* as a "commando raid on ... what conventional criticism had been content to regard as ineffable," but "it turned out that his main principles had been quietly absorbed into the canon of modern literary criticism." Defines Empson's method as "an intuitive grasp of the work, followed by an analytical attempt to show how the intuition was arrived at," and stresses Empson's belief that "the reaction in the reader's mind reconstitutes the reaction in the mind of the author at the time of creation." Although the symbolism of Empson's analytical machinery in *Complex Words* is "ill-chosen and unmemorable," the essays are "brilliant and deeply thought." Judges Empson's work as "immensely important," but so rich that "literary studies must go on digesting it for some time."

I53 Hyman, Stanley Edgar. "William Empson and Categorical Criticism." *The Armed Vision: A Study in the Methods of Modern Literary Criticism.* New York: Vintage Books, 1955. Pp. 237-77.

Ranks Empson among the best critics of his day, judging *Some Versions of Pastoral*--"implicitly Marxist throughout"--his best work. The seven chapters of *Some Versions of Pastoral* are "simply seven versions of pastoral poetry." Asserts that "Empson's pastoral category is the artificial cult of simplicity, the literary equivalent of Marie Antoinette and her ladies-in-waiting cavorting on the greensward dressed as milkmaids." Identifies Darwin and Frazer, as well as Marx and Freud, as influences on *Some Versions of Pastoral*; points to works by William Hazlitt and Georg Brandes as antecedents of Empson's use of pastoral, and places Empson in a tradition of categorical criticism beginning in eighteenth-century England. Sketches Empson's influence on other critics such as Blackmur (influenced "greatly" by *Seven Types*), Burke (who "refers frequently and approvingly to Empson") and, most importantly, Brooks and Ransom. A valuable essay, rich in summary and quotation from *Seven Types* and *Some Versions of Pastoral*.

I54 Jensen, James. "The Construction of *Seven Types of Ambiguity*." *Modern Language Quarterly* 27 (September, 1966), pp. 243-59.

Begins with the assumption that *Seven Types* fails "to rationalize and to implement a coherently workable critical theory" and hypothesizes as to why "The genius of the book is at odds with its structure, yet the structure imposes itself before anything else...." In brief, the answer suggested is that Empson took his method of close reading from Riding and Graves but that the subjectivity of the Riding-Graves approach dismayed the tutor Richards, whose insistence "that an objective structure be imposed on the book would have been based on his belief that by this means alone could it be saved from an unredeemed act of egoism." Jensen fluently composes a gross outline: "At the start, then, there was a short burst of critical energy which generated the core of the book; this was followed by a longer stage of supervised writing and planning, when, among other things, the 'types' scheme was probably settled upon and refined; then came a period preceding publication when the manuscript was put in final form by Empson alone." An extremely well written essay with stimulating insights such as this comment on *Seven Types*: "Its ungainliness is un-Ricardian: instead of moving toward rational clarification by carefully unscrambling submerged and ill-defined meanings, the impetus of the whole types scheme is toward further complexity, toward a greater and greater involvement in emotive detail." (For responses by Empson, Graves, and Richards that accompany the article, see G71, L11, L27, and M27.)

I55 Jensen, James. "Some Ambiguous Preliminaries: Empson in *The Granta*." *Criticism: A Quarterly for Literature and the Arts* 8 (Fall, 1966), pp. 349-61.

Discerns in Empson's *Granta* reviews a search for a method of critical synthesis finally satisfied by his reading of Riding and Graves's *A Survey of Modernist Poetry* (1927) and demonstrated for the first time in his review of Lady Murasaki's *Blue Trousers* (see F15). Ends with an important insight: "Yet Empson has consistently been aware of the claims of both the rational and non-rational poles of literary experience, of their ambiguous ability to interpenetrate and thereby to compromise or enhance each other. And it is just this consciousness, this capability of working both the objective and subjective sides of the track, which constitutes the essential and considerable value of his critical example."

(*The Granta* was the Cambridge University student magazine, which got its name from the Sanskrit word used by Sikhs for their holy scriptures.)

I56 Juhl, P.D. "Empson on Housman." *Interpretation: An Essay in the Philosophy of Literary Criticism*. Princeton: Princeton University Press, 1980. Pp. 169-75.

Explores Empson's judgment that Housman's "With seeds the sowers scatter" is "one of his finest poems" even though its meaning seems to him "plainly untrue," concluding that "Empson's interpretation does depend on assumptions about the real Housman's beliefs."

I57 Kenner, Hugh. "Alice in Empsonland." Review of *The Structure of Complex Words*. *Hudson Review* 5 (1952), pp. 137-44.

Finds *Complex Words* "disappointing," a collection of "disjunct" essays that are less interesting than the theory itself, which has more rigor than Empson's concept of ambiguity. Summarizes concisely the critical apparatus of *Complex Words* (this summary is quoted in the annotation of A3), judging it neat enough but wanting in usefulness for the critic. Empson's method of analysis of key words is inadequate in opening up long poems and ineffective with concrete images. Behind Empson's approach to criticism lies an assumption that words are subjective, an assumption that helps generate a criticism of personal satisfaction. Kenner admires Empson's enthusiasm and mental agility, especially in *Seven Types*, but declares that *Complex Words* is a futile work: "he has accommodated himself at length to his own image of the Victorian scientist, who was 'believed to have discovered a new kind of Roman virtue,' and whom the public could always surprise, as Alice did the White Knight, obliviously head down in his suit of armor, hung with bellows and beehives, 'patiently labouring at his absurd but fruitful conceptions.'"

I57a Kenner, Hugh. "Alice in Empsonland." *Gnomon: Essays on Contemporary Literature*. New York: McDowell, Obolensky, 1958. Pp. 249-62.

Reprint of I57.

I58 Kris, Ernst, and Abraham Kaplan. "Aesthetic Ambiguity." *Psychoanalytic Explorations in Art*. New York: International Universities Press, 1952. Pp. 243-64.

Frequent reference made to Empson as the authors attempt to (1) "differentiate more closely the kind of ambiguity characteristic of poetry from that found in nonpoetic language"; (2) develop the conception of art as a process of communication and re-creation, in which ambiguity plays a central role; and (3) "make explicit the standards of interpretation of ambiguity."

I59 Leavis, F.R. *New Bearings in English Poetry*. London: Chatto and Windus, 1942.

Devotes four pages to Empson in an epilogue, praising his "remarkable" poems in *Cambridge Poetry 1929*. Asserts that Empson's poetry was made possible by the re-orientation to the Metaphysicals produced by Eliot, and describes it as "very original" and "rich" but preoccupied with technique and sometimes "unjustifiably" difficult.

I60 Lemon, Lee. *The Partial Critics*. New York: Oxford University Press, 1965.

Finds that modern critics fail to take complete account of works they study. Praises Empson's handling of ambiguities (pp. 130-34), but feels that Empson's approach is often irresponsible in that it does not cope with the whole work.

I61 Linneman, M. Rose Ann, S.S.N.D. "Donne as Catalyst in the Poetry of Elinor Wylie, Wallace Stevens, Herbert Read, and William Empson." *Xavier University Studies* 1 (1962), pp. 264-72.

Empson's poetry "tags him the brilliant smart-alec because it reflects more of a self-conscious intellectualism and a less genuine emotionalism than the poetry of Donne."

I62 Maxwell-Mahon, W.D. "The Divided Glancer: A Comment on William Empson." *English Studies in Africa* 11 (1968), pp. 35-41.

Examines several Empson poems in terms of their expression of ambiguity. "His use of ambiguity is not a deliberate obscurity contrived to mirror the confused state of society, it is an argumentative complexity of expression that indicates an unresolved spiritual conflict, a conflict between the man who feels and the man who thinks."

I63 Maxwell-Mahon, W.D. "The Early Poetry of William Empson." *Unisa English Studies* 10, 1 (1972), pp. 12-22.

I64 Maxwell-Mahon, W.D. "William Empson: The Development of an Idiom." *Unisa English Studies* 8 (March, 1970), pp. 24-6.

I65 McLuhan, H.M. "Poetic *vs.* Rhetorical Exegesis: The Case for Leavis Against Richards and Empson." *Sewanee Review* 52 (Spring, 1944), pp. 266-76.

Assumes that prose writers have intentions toward an audience whereas poets do not. Prose, or rhetorical, works have action as their goal, but a "poetic work is an action produced for the sake of contemplation." The analytical approaches of Richards and Empson, although effective in dealing with rhetoric and valuable in having made art "respectable and redoubtable once more for all intelligent men," offer no evaluation, and thus Leavis's criticism has a "superior relevance." Concludes that "Where Mr. Leavis sees the function of poetry as education or nourishment of the affections, Richards and Empson tend to regard it pragmatically and rhetorically as a means of impinging on a particular situation."

I66 Meller, Horst. "William Empson." In *Englische Dichter der Moderne: Ihr Leben und Werk,* eds. Rudolf Suhnel and Dieter Riesner. Berlin: Schmidt, 1971. Pp. 474-88.

I67 Meller, Horst. "William Empsons 'Arachne': Eine Interpretation." *Archiv* 201 (1964-65), pp. 185-90.

I68 Meller, Horst. "William Empson: 'This Last Pain.'" *Zeitgenössische englische Dichtung* I, ed. H. Meller. Frankfurt, 1966. Pp. 80-88.

I69 Mercer, Peter, and Roger Fowler. "Criticism and the Language of Literature: Some Traditions and Trends in Great Britain. *Style* 3 (1969), pp. 45-72.

See I31, under Fowler, Roger.

I70 Miller, Karl. "Empson Agonistes." In *William Empson: The Man and His Work*, ed. Roma Gill. London and Boston: Routledge and Kegan Paul, 1974. Pp. 41-8.

Empson once wrote reviews for the *New Statesman* when Miller was its literary editor. Miller says Empson is a "just and kind man" and believes that "it can, after all, be assumed that his teachings will have a long run, that they will be mediated, and made doctrinal, to a nation that has not yet come into being."

I71 Ogoshi, Inzo. "Kokoru no Futatsu no Michi no--Empson no Saisetsu." *Eigo Seinen* (Tokyo) 116 (1970), pp. 192-3.

Translates as "Empson Reconsidered."

I72 Olson, Elder. "William Empson, Contemporary Criticism and Poetic Diction." *Modern Philology* 47 (May, 1950), pp. 222-52.

Broad attack on the New Criticism, with Empson identified as one of its "principal exponents." Accuses Empson of being "utterly innocent of any knowledge of the history of criticism" and of failing to discriminate between meaning and inference, thus producing a criticism that identifies the poem with its diction. The display of dictionary definitions in Empson's work is therefore an absurd emphasis on one of the least important parts of a poem.

I72a Olson, Elder. "William Empson, Contemporary Criticism and Poetic Diction." In *Critics and Criticism: Ancient and Modern*, ed. R.S. Crane. Chicago: University of Chicago Press, 1952. Pp. 45-82.

Reprint of I72.

I72b Olson, Elder. "William Empson, Contemporary Criticism and Poetic Diction." *On Value Judgments in the Arts and Other Essays*. Chicago and London: University of Chicago Press, 1976. Pp. 118-56.

Reprint of I72.

I73 Ormerod, David. "Empson's 'Invitation to Juno.'" *Explicator* 25 (October, 1966), Item 13.

I74 Otten, Kurt. "William Empson: 'This Last Pain.'" *Die moderne englische Lyrik: Interpretationen*, ed. Horst Oppel. Berlin, 1976. Pp. 185-92.

I75 Parker, William Riley. *Milton: A Biography*. 2 vols. Oxford: Clarendon Press, 1968.

Pages 964-6 constitute a retort to Empson's account in *Milton's God* (A4) of the charge that Milton had included a forged prayer in an edition of *Eikon Basilike*. The "main facts" behind the story are sketched and a bibliography provided of the ensuing letters to *TLS* and Empson's answers.

I76 Pinsker, Sanford. "Finite but Unbounded: The Poetic World of William Empson." *University of Windsor Review* 3 (Fall, 1967), pp. 88-96.

Explores the possible meanings of several of Empson's poems.

I77 Praz, Mario. "Historical and Evaluative Criticism." In *Literary History and Literary Criticism*, ed. Leon Edel. New York: New York University Press, 1964. Pp. 65-77.

A general discussion of shifting attitudes in criticism produces an intriguing comparison:

"The same type of attention spellbound by magnified minutiae which we find in Salvador Dali's paintings is witnessed in Empson's explorations ... of all possible meanings of words and the consequent opening of strange perspectives in the pages of classics: these, then, acquire a 'tension,' a dramatic irony which is not unlike certain effects of surrealism. Empson's interest in misprints, which he finds illuminating because according to him they suggest buried meanings, could be paralleled in the surrealist's deliberate cult of solecisms in the shape of objects (limp clocks, flexible celloes, telephone receivers used as electric stoves, and so on)."

I78 Raimondi, Ezio. "La critica simbolica." *Modern Language Notes* 84 (1969), pp. 1-15.

Brief mention of Empson, whose notion of complex words is seen as a forerunner of the systems of imagery G. Wilson Knight develops in a criticism "midway between the 'New Criticism' and Spitzerian philology."

I78a Raimondi, Ezio. "Symbolic Criticism." Translated by Catherine and Richard Macksey. In *Velocities of Change: Critical Essays from MLN*, ed. Richard Macksey. Baltimore and London: Johns Hopkins University Press, 1974. Pp. 118-37.

Reprint in translation of I78. Includes "Bibliographic Note" by the editor.

I79 Raine, Kathleen. *Defending Ancient Springs*. London: Oxford University Press, 1967.

Admires Empson's brilliance but finds his view of life inadequate. "What William Empson ... gave his generation was a theory of poetry consistent with the positivist philosophy which flourished in Cambridge...." But "he fails to consider that resonance which may be present within an image of apparent simplicity, setting into vibration planes of reality and of consciousness other than that of the sensible world" (p. 107). (See also Miss Raine's memoir of her university days with Empson in M42.)

I80 Ransom, John Crowe. "Mr. Empson's Muddles." *Southern Review* 4 (July, 1938-April, 1939), pp. 322-39.

An excellent analysis, essentially a discussion of the essays in *Some Versions of Pastoral*. Defines his uneasiness about Empson: "I am afraid of the rise of a doctrine which would teach that the poem is what we make it." Identifies "two separate situations" recognized by Empson "with respect to the poet-expositor relation": that in which the poet was aware of the meanings exposited and that in which "some of them came out of his unconscious mind." Defines the elucidation of conscious meanings as "logical," that of unconscious meanings as "psychological"; and sees Empson's psychological criticism as representing "the reading of the poet's muddled mind by some later, freer, and more self-conscious mind." Thinks that Empson puts so much pressure on language that "He almost makes of poetry a cryptogram." Judges the essay on Alice as definitive, and that on Milton and Bentley as nearly as good, although rejecting Empson's "almost fanatical devotion to puns." Perceives "too sharp angles, and too many of them" in the reading of Shakespeare's Sonnet XCIV, and condemns the essay on Marvell's "The Garden" as "the most extreme example of what I regard as Mr. Empson's almost inveterate habit of over-reading poetry." Stresses Empson's debt to I.A. Richards for his psychological view of poetry, which "argues that the end of poetry is the 'satisfaction' of a subject (the poet, and his beneficiary the reader), and not the affirmation of an object." Asserts that "the poetic act if it is important remains, ideally at least, an act of the same order as the religious act: a metaphysical affirmation." Denies that all muddles are the same, maintaining that some complications "support and enforce a central meaning and do not diffuse it or dissolve it."

I81

Ransom, John Crowe. *The New Criticism*. Norfolk, Connecticut: New Directions, 1941. Pp. 101-31.

Discusses Empson at the end of a long chapter

on Richards, commenting only on *Seven Types*, which is quoted at length (the analyses of passages from Sidney's *Arcadia*, "Tintern Abbey," and Shakespeare's Sonnet 73). Praises the "extreme intelligence" of Empson's commentaries. "Richards and Empson have spread quickly. That is a principal reason why I think it is time to identify a powerful intellectual movement that deserves to be called a new criticism." Finds in the exhaustive analysis of Sonnet 73 a lack of attention to structure: "It seems to me extremely important to recognize and approve such logical structure as a poem may have; its texture of meanings should find a structure to attach itself to. The poets are not quite irresponsible, and the readers should not be more irresponsible than the poets."

I82 Rawson, C.J. "Professor Empson's *Tom Jones*." *Notes and Queries* 204, n.s. VI (1959), pp. 400-404.

Describes Empson's essay on *Tom Jones* as a "classic reappraisal" but rejects as "misleading" the ironic tone Empson attributes to the novel. (See D55.)

I82a Rawson, C.J. "Professor Empson's *Tom Jones*." In *Henry Fielding's "Tom Jones." A Casebook*, ed. Neil Compton. London: Macmillan, 1972. Pp. 173-81.

Reprint of I82.

I83 Richards, I.A. "Semantic Frontiersman." In *William Empson: The Man and His Work*, ed. Roma Gill. London and Boston: 1974, Pp. 98-108.

Maintains of Empson that "*at his best* he is able to point out, describe, and make evident co-operations and interactions among meanings on a scale and with a subtlety and resource not to be found in previous critics." Complains of the two theoretical opening chapters of *Complex Words* that Empson's "percipiences ... are incommensurably more refined than the clumsy terms through which he is ... trying to control and expound them."

I84 Ricks, Christopher. "Empson's Poetry." In *William Empson: The Man and His Work*, ed. Roma Gill. London and Boston: Routledge and Kegan Paul, 1974. Pp. 145-207.

In preparing for his main thesis, Ricks stresses the importance to Empson of story, of the tension of life's contradictions, and of decision-making. Then he argues by reference to Empson's works "that the complex of thinking and feeling involved in begetting--man's desire to raise posterity--is 'the right handle to take hold of the bundle', or at any rate a right handle, in considering Empson's poems." Gives close attention to a number of poems, including "To an Old Lady," "The Ants," "Value Is in Activity," "Camping Out," "Letter II," "Arachne," "The Scales," "Homage to the British Museum," "Note on Local "Flora," "Missing Dates," "The Teasers," "Thanks for a Wedding Present," and "Chinese Ballad."
"I believe that almost all of Empson's poems have to do with the way in which we do or do not short-circuit life."

I85 Righter, William. *Logic and Criticism*. London: Routledge and Kegan Paul, 1963. Pp. 100-107.

Criticizes the logic of *Seven Types*, finding that ambiguity is used obscurely as a "conceptual bridge" between linguistics and psychology. "Yet the causal relation is never particularly emphasized. It is almost as if it is assumed that the word ambiguity simply stands for the necessary bridge, that having introduced it the connection is complete, and that having shown the many-levelled complexity of language, and the many-levelled complexity of a human being, that an explanation is complete. It is then enough to develop the seven varieties." (See I87.)

I86 Romhild, Lars P. "En paradoxal kritiker: Empson." *Laesere: Antikler og foredrag* (Munksgaardserien 42). Copenhagen: Munksgaard, 1971. Pp. 70-82.

I87 Ruthven, K.K. "The Pluralistic Theory of Meaning." *Critical Assumptions*. London and New York: Cambridge University Press, 1979. Pp. 155-7.

Defends Empson against Righter's criticism of

the logic in *Seven Types*: "But taking all this into account, there is no doubt that a copy of Empson's book (suitably re-titled *'N' types of plurisignation*, to quieten one sort of objector) can do more than any comparable study to convince one of the sheer unlikelihood that any work of literature can have one meaning and one meaning only." (See I85.)

I88 Sale, Roger. "The Achievement of William Empson." *Hudson Review* 19 (Autumn, 1966), pp. 369-90.

A preliminary version of H8.

I89 Schultz, Fred C. "Apian Imagery in Empson's 'To an Old Lady.'" *Notes on Contemporary Literature* 4, 2 (1974), pp. 5-7.

I90 Sleight, Richard. "Mr. Empson's Complex Words." *Criticism* 2 (1952), pp. 325-37.

Judges the machinery of Empson's equations "perplexing at first" and thinks that "They perhaps need a special type of mind to handle them adequately." Perceives that Empson's method runs into trouble in trying to explain the "mostly unconscious methods used by people to communicate verbally" and concludes that "Trying to explain irrationality by conscious thought-processes usually only succeeds in underlining its irrational character." Although *Complex Words* is often "Irritating, difficult and wrong-headed," it is "unquestionably the most important contribution to critical theory since *The Sacred Wood*."

I91 Sparrow, John. "Incoherence." *Sense and Poetry*. New Haven: Yale University Press, 1934. Pp. 51-70.

The imagery in "The Scales" obscures rather than illuminates the skeleton of thought.

I92 Spector, Robert. "Form and Content in Empson's 'Missing Dates.'" *Modern Language Notes* 74 (April, 1959), pp. 310-311.

I93 Stock, A.G. "*New Signatures* in Retrospect." In *William Empson: The Man and His Work*, ed. Roma Gill. London and Boston: Routledge and Kegan Paul, 1974. Pp. 126-44.

Includes comments on "This Last Pain" and "Note on Local Flora."

I94 Strickland, Geoffrey. "The Criticism of William Empson." *Mandrake* 2 (Autumn-Winter, 1954-55), pp. 320-31.

Indicts Empson for pursuing interpretation at the expense of judgment: "It is impossible to conceive the organic growth of the sensibility without its continuity of judgment. It is equally impossible to think of true critical flexibility without critical resistance." One of the most acute commentaries on Empson's criticism. (See G44.)

I95 Strickland, Geoffrey. "The Poetry of William Empson." *Mandrake* 2 (Autumn-Winter, 1954-55), pp. 245-55.

Rejects the identification of Empson's verse with that of Donne: "Its distinction seems to be that ... he comes near to the achievement, not of Donne or Marvell, but of the Swift of the digressions in *Tale of a Tub*...." Despite its example as a "valuable discipline of unsentimental thought," Empson's poetry displays the "inadequacies of a technique used as a substitute for intelligent self-realisation."

I96 Thurley, Geoffrey. "'Partial Fires': Empson's Poetry." *The Ironic Harvest: English Poetry in the Twentieth Century*. New York: St. Martin's Press, 1974. Pp. 38-53.

Thurley's own summary aptly gives the gist of his essay: "The 'partial fires' of Empson's poem are partial because the philosophical strategy behind all Empson's thought, as behind the whole intellectualist tradition, insisted upon a kind of constitutional ambivalence, a reverence for the ambiguous, the undecided, the ironically qualified. Ambiguity suggests that things are not as they seem, and probably the reverse of what we think; to be on the safe side we had better hedge our bets, qualify our utterance so that we cannot be caught out (caught out actually saying something, presumably)."

I97 Tillotson, Geoffrey. *Essays in Criticism and Research*. Cambridge: Cambridge University Press, 1942. Pp. xvi-xvii.

Snide dismissal of Empson's "unsatisfactory" criticism.

I98 Tindall, William York. *Forces in Modern British Literature: 1885-1946*. New York: Alfred A. Knopf, 1947.

Derides Empson's prose as "unattractive" and his division of ambiguity into seven types as "unnecessary and pretentious," but admits that "his exemplary analyses are exemplary." On the poetry: "As puzzles for explicators Empson composed the excellent, compressed, ambiguous poems...."

I99 Touster, Saul. "Empson's Legal Fiction." *The Review: A Magazine* of Poetry and Criticism (June, 1963), pp. 45-8.

Reads "Legal Fiction" as a parable of the "terrifying" ability of Law to "utilize the coercive power of the state" in bringing everyone under its reign of order and destroying each individual's uniqueness. "Geometry is another kind of ordering device, comparable to law, that wipes away distinctions, destroys uniqueness, constricts the chaotic and coarse flow of ideas into a Puritanic regularity."

I100 Untermeyer, Louis. *Lives of the Poets*. New York: Simon and Schuster, 1959.

Praises Empson as poet for his "intellectual" approach and "free use of scientific as well as classical allusions," but laments his "too great a value on erudition, on form instead of substance, technique instead of tone, manner instead of content."

I101 Wain, John. "Ambiguous Gifts: Notes on the Poetry of William Empson." *Penguin New Writing*. Harmondsworth: Penguin, 1949.

Notes Empson's success in using imagery from science and technology in developing the general meaning of a poem. Suggests the subject of "The Teasers" is "our inward afflictions and aspirations." Links Empson to the Metaphysicals in his willingness to let his conceits unfold at length, and admires the "passion, logic, and formal beauty" of Empson's poetry.

I101a Wain, John. "Ambiguous Gifts: Notes on the Poetry of William Empson." *Preliminary Essays*. London: Macmillan; New York: St, Martin's Press, 1957. Pp. 169-80.

Reprint of I101.

I102 Wain, John. "The Poetic Mind of William Empson." *Lugano Review* (Autumn, 1976), pp. 95-114, 118.

Offers provocative explications of several Empson poems, finding the poetry "difficult because of his highly idiosyncratic idiom, an idiom that pays great dividends in flavour and memorability"; argues convincingly the case for Frazer as an important influence on Empson, especially in *Some Versions of Pastoral*; defends the achievement of *The Gathering Storm*, judging it to be less different from the earlier poems than often claimed; discusses *Milton's God* sympathetically and says that "Empson's view of Christianity is interesting but not the only one." Excellent, wide-ranging discussion.

I102a Wain, John. "The Poetry of William Empson." *Professing Poetry*. New York: Viking Press, 1978. Pp. 177-223.

Reprint of I102.

I103 Waldock, A.J.A. *"Paradise Lost" and Its Critics*. London: Cambridge University Press, 1947.

Rejects (pp. 87-88) Empson's reading (*Some*

Versions of Pastoral, p. 168) of *Paradise Lost*, IV, ll. 368-76, but admits that the tone of ll. 374-6 takes on a "more direct eloquence than is really appropriate." Also rejects (pp. 140-43) Empson's interpretation (*Some Versions of Pastoral*, pp. 170-2) of the similes in *Paradise Lost*, II, ll. 625-34, and IV, ll. 967-77. "The effort to find continuous relevance in Milton's similes may succeed on occasion, but it is an effort ... that can easily overreach itself."

I103a Waldock, A.J.A. *"Paradise Lost" and Its Critics*. Gloucester, Massachusetts: Peter Smith, 1959.

Reprint of I103.

I104 Waseda Daigaku Empson Kenkynkai. *Empson Nyumon*. Tokyo: Hokuseido, 1972.

Translates as "Introduction to William Empson."

I105 Watson, George. *The Literary Critics: A Study of English Descriptive Criticism*. Harmondsworth and Baltimore: Penguin Books, 1962. Pp. 202-8.

Places Empson in the "neo-critical" movement in England in the twenties, of which Eliot is "part pioneer, part sceptic," Richards is creator of a "ramshackle aesthetic," and Empson is Richards's "greatest disciple." *Seven Types* and *Some Versions of Pastoral* exemplify the two main thrusts of New Criticism: *Seven Types* in its close verbal analyses, and *Some Versions of Pastoral* in its organic studies of whole works. (The first essay of *Some Versions of Pastoral* is "a manifesto for a Socialist literature, this, and Empson's unique excursion into legislative literature.") *Complex Words* approaches "historicism" from a "literary angle," and *Milton's God* is "magnificently vituperative." Judges Empson the first to systematize close verbal analysis, and defends him despite his occasional "rashness" against Eliot's dismissal of the technique. The main limitations of verbal analysis--its absorption in brief works or passages and its invitation to preciosity--

are "dangers" Empson has generally worked around. The passion of Empson's work acquits him of any charge of mere flashiness. A brief but judicious appraisal.

I105a Watson, George. *The Literary Critics: A Study of English Descriptive Criticism.* 2nd ed. Totowa, New Jersey: Rowman and Littlefield, 1973.

Second edition of I105.

I106 Wellek, René. "The Main Trends of Twentieth-Century Criticism." *Yale Review* 51 (1961), pp. 102-18.

Disposes of Empson in two sentences: "*Seven Types of Ambiguity* (1930) pursues to the farthest ends the implications, poetic and social, of difficult, witty, metaphorical poetry by a method of verbal analysis which often loses all contact with the text and indulges in private associations. In his later books Empson combined this semantic analysis with ideas drawn from psychoanalysis and Marxism, and recently he has practically left the realm of literary criticism for a special kind of linguistic analysis which is often only a pretext for the fireworks of his wit and recondite ingenuity."

I106a Wellek, René. "The Main Trends of Twentieth-Century Criticism." In Wellek's *Concepts of Criticism*, ed. Stephen G. Nichols, Jr. New Haven and London: Yale University Press, 1963. Pp. 344-64.

Reprint of I106.

I107 Wetherill, P.M. *The Literary Text: An Examination of Critical Methods.* Berkeley and Los Angeles: University of California Press, 1974.

Careful analysis of critical approaches to the following topics: Sounds, Grammar, Meaning, Style, Counting, Construction, and Sequence. Numerous references to *Seven Types* and *Complex Words*. Of *Seven Types*: "the initial premise ... is considerably more important than the categories he worked out." Of *Complex Words*: "an outstanding example of what the examination of individual words can achieve in literary criticism." Extremely useful bibliography of almost 800 items.

I108 Wimsatt, William K., Jr., and Cleanth Brooks. *Literary Criticism: A Short History*. New York: Alfred A. Knopf, 1957.

See under Brooks, Cleanth. Item I12.

I109 Winter, Helmut. "William Empson." *Literaturtheorie und Literaturkritik*. Bern and Munich: Francke Verlag; Düsseldorf: August Bagel Verlag, 1974. Pp. 133-7.

Brief account of Empson's first three volumes of criticism.

J

REVIEWS OF WORKS BY EMPSON

J1 Anonymous. "Book Notes: *Seven Types of Ambiguity.*" *New Republic* 66 (March 11, 1931), p. 107.

"Stimulating but difficult reading."

J2 Bradbrook, Muriel C. "The Criticism of William Empson." *Scrutiny* 2 (1933-34), pp. 253-7.

Appreciates Empson's intelligence and sensitivity, but faults him for the lack in *Seven Types* of "judgment, a sense of relative values without which criticism is no more than a game for the intelligent and an emotional showerbath."

J3 Cox, R.G. "Ambiguity Revised." Review of *Seven Types*, 2nd ed. *Scrutiny* 15 (1947-48), pp. 148-52.

Criticizes *Seven Types* for its lack of discrimination and value judgments and for extravagance in interpretation. "On those critics who have been anxious to achieve a reputation for keeping up to date while lacking the kind of sensibility and intelligence required for genuinely original analysis, Mr. Empson's influence has made for a relaxation of discipline and has contributed to various kinds of irresponsible eccentricity."

J4 Leavis, F.R. "Empson's Criticism." Review of *Seven Types. Cambridge Review* (January 16, 1931.

Praises *Seven Types* as "that rare thing, a critical work of the first order" although Empson is sometimes "apt to be a little too ingenious in detecting ambiguities."

J4a Leavis, F.R. "Empson's Criticism." In Eric Homberger, William Janeway, and Simon Schama, eds. *The Cambridge Mind*. Boston: Little, Brown; London: Jonathan Cape, 1970. Pp. 256-60.

Reprint of J4.

J5 Murry, John Middleton. "William Empson's *Seven Types of Ambiguity*." *TLS* (December 18, 1930).

Questions the value of Empson's critical method on grounds that the "organic whole" of a poem cannot be analyzed, and concludes that *Seven Types* "obscures rather than explains."

J5a Murry, John Middleton. "William Empson's *Seven Types of Ambiguity*." *Poets, Critics, Mystics: A Selection of Criticisms Written Between 1919 and 1955 by John Middleton Murry*, ed. Richard Rees. Carbondale: Southern Illinois University Press; London: Feffer and Simons, 1970. Pp. 78-82.

Reprint of J5.

J6 Rosenburg, Harold. Review of *Seven Types of Ambiguity*. *The Symposium* 2 (July, 1931), pp. 412-18.

Unsympathetic. Finds that Empson's approach differs from that of Riding and Graves in that he multiplies meanings whereas they believed that "there is one precise idea or emotion which a poem is meant to communicate." Argues that Freudian insights are misused in the analyses: "It follows that an 'interpretation' finds its limitation in some unity to which details however gathered are referred; while an 'analysis' must be restricted to logical and reasonable derivations. Thus fenced, these processes can go on side by side without either leading the other astray."

J7 Smith, James. Review of *Seven Types of Ambiguity*. *Criterion* 10 (July, 1931), pp. 738-42.

Makes the following criticisms: (1) the definition of ambiguity is too vague; (2) many analyses have no properly critical conclusion; (3) analyses of mental conflicts in an author's mind are invalid; (4) it is not clear whether the ambiguities are those inherent in life, or are literary devices; (5) the examples of drama are irrelevant to English poetry.

"Mr. Empson rides with all the impedimenta of the White Knight, and in choice of attack shows the ardour of Don Quixote."

J8 Burke, Kenneth. "Exceptional Book." Review of *English Pastoral Poetry*. *New Republic* 95 (May 25, 1938), p. 81.

Identifies Empson as "an offshoot of I.A. Richards" and asserts that his "feeling for literature as a social manifestation is acute, fertile and well documented," but admits that "often his perceptions are too refined, leading him into a welter of observations that suffer from lack of selectivity and drive." *English Pastoral Poetry* (the American title of *Some Versions of Pastoral*) retains the "liquidity" of *Seven Types*, and its "Marxist emphasis" gives it a "social base of reference." (See J9.)

J8a Burke, Kenneth. "Exceptional Book." *Philosophy of Literary Form: Studies in Symbolic Action*. Baton Rouge: Louisiana State University Press, 1941. Pp. 424-6.

Reprint of J8.

J9 Burke, Kenneth. "Exceptional Improvisation." Review of *Some Versions of Pastoral*. *Poetry* 49 (March, 1937), pp. 347-50.

Interprets "pastoral" as "that subtle reversal of values whereby the last become first," elevating "humble rustics, criminals, children, and fools." Although Empson is regarded as "inclined to self-indulgence," *Some Versions of Pastoral* is judged as "one of the keenest, most independent, and most imaginative books of criticism" of its period, with many excellent "incidental passages" such as the "profoundly Marxist analysis" of Gray's "Elegy." (See J8.)

J9a Burke, Kenneth. "Exceptional Improvisation." *Philosophy of Literary Form: Studies in Symbolic Action*. Baton Rouge: Louisiana State University Press, 1941. Pp. 422-4.

Reprint of J9.

J10 Hawkins, Desmond. "Illuminated Texts." Review of *Some Versions of Pastoral*. *Spectator* 95 (November 15, 1935), p. 828.

"Mr. Empson's book ranks among the most stimulating criticism of recent years."

J11 Hunter, Guy. "Science and Magic." Review of *Some Versions of Pastoral*. *The London Mercury* 33 (1935-36), p. 447.

Praises Empson's fusion in *Some Versions of Pastoral* of a mythical definition of literature with a social one.

J12 Mason, H.A. "William Empson's Criticism." Review of *Some Versions of Pastoral*. *Scrutiny* 4 (1935-36), pp. 431-4.

Calls "Proletarian Literature" the best essay in a volume that "lacks first of all the vigour and exuberance of the earlier book." Concludes that "*Some Versions of Pastoral* would not make a fit companion volume to *Seven Types* on the shelves of the beginner in criticism."

J13 Mizener, Arthur. "The Truest Poetrie." Review of *English Pastoral Poetry*. *Partisan Review* 5 (June, 1938), pp. 57-60.

Praises this study because "it deals with the past in terms which make it available to the present." Explains that Empson assumes a work to be an "elaborate metaphor," or "the objective correlative of the author's thought and feeling"; so that the critic's job is "to analyze the structure of the metaphor" and demonstrate "why the age which produced the work of art in question felt this complex but unified attitude to be important." Empson himself uses a pastoral device: "he is the revolutionary critic in the guise of a correspondent of *The Times Literary Supplement.*" But in this guise he annoys the reader by explaining too little; and the definition of proletarian literature is too broad: "it is quite as good as a definition of contemporary literature in general." The final assessment of the book is high: "Not only is its method the critical elaboration most useful for our day but its practical criticism is richer and more pertinent than that of any book which comes to mind. Mr. Empson's manner is deceptive and sometimes annoying but the reader's reward for bearing with him will more than repay the effort it may cost him."

J14 Cooke, Fletcher. "*Poems*, by Empson." *The Granta* (October 9, 1935), p. 17.

J15 MacNeice, Louis. "Mr. Empson As a Poet." Review of *Poems*. *New Verse* No. 16 (August-September, 1935), pp. 17-18.

Even though Empson is "a great hand at words, his syntax arrests, and he can manage the significant pun," still "there is not enough blood and sweat in him." "The clever fellows must wait to show off some other day."

J16 Mason, H.A. "William Empson's Verse." Review of *Poems*. *Scrutiny* 4 (1935-36), pp. 302-4.

"But the present volume enables us to state that the number of poems which justify his high reputation is extremely small and almost wholly confined to poems written before 1929."

J17 Richards, I.A. "The Poetry of William Empson." Review of *Poems*. *Cambridge Review* (February 14, 1936).

Discovers lines that "resound with an extraordinary and inexplicable passion" in this "superlative book of riddles." "I hope he will reduce the compression, be content to score much less than a possible of puns, even when the feat is most tempting, and try a subject with more resistance to manipulation."

J17a Richards, I.A. "The Poetry of William Empson." In Eric Homberger, William Janeway, and Simon Schama, eds. *The Cambridge Mind*. Boston: Little, Brown; London: Jonathan Cape, 1970. Pp. 260-2.

Reprint of J17. Has an excellent photograph of Empson with a foot-long cigarette holder.

J18 Roberts, Michael. "A Metaphysical Poet." Review of *Poems*. *The London Mercury* 32 (August, 1935), pp. 387-9.

One of the more sympathetic reviews of *Poems*.

J19 Sitwell, Edith. "Four New Poets." Review of *Poems*. *The London Mercury* 33 (1935-36), pp. 383-90.

Complains that "whilst his language is so important and significant that it is the blood and bone of the poems, his rhythms are clumsy, for the most part."

J20 Anonymous. "Puzzles in Verse: The Cult of Ambiguity." Review of *The Gathering Storm*. *TLS* 39 (October 12, 1940), p. 522.

Decides that "the prevailing impression they still leave is one of intricate obscurity."

J21 Mellers, W.H. "Cats in Air-Pumps." Review of *The Gathering Storm*. *Scrutiny* 9 (December, 1940), pp. 290-3.

Judges the poems "essentially obscure."

J22 Brooks, Cleanth. "Hits and Misses." Review of *The Structure of Complex Words*. *Kenyon Review* 14 (1952), pp. 669-78.

Locates Empson "on the borderland of linguistics and literary criticism." Distinguishes Empson's equations (they derive from the history of the language) from ambiguities ("the result of the stylizing of language by an individual writer"). Judges the first chapter on Sense and Emotion as "perhaps the most interesting and rewarding" but confides that, "If I have any general quarrel with Empson, it is that in his own later literary criticism he does not always abide by the consequences of a Cognitive view of poetry." The chapter on "Wit in the *Essay on Criticism*" is "brilliant and convincing," but the equations could be just as well seen as ambiguities and the essay could just as appropriately have been included in *Seven Types*. Provides a fundamental objection: "the classification is not relevant to the value of the criticism." The essay on *all* in *Paradise Lost* only reveals Empson's prejudice against Milton's theology. Expresses satisfaction with Empson's interest in the author's intention and the audience's response, but protests that Empson is sloppy in his treatment of these elements in his analyses. Furthermore, his inattention to relevance leads Empson to "some very weird readings." Empson is an "incorrigible amateur," and *Complex Words*, although a "kind of ragbag," is "provocative and seminal."

J23 Cohen, J.M. "On Portmanteau Words." Review of *The Structure of Complex Words*. *Spectator* 187 (September 21, 1951), p. 372.

Even though the discoveries in *Complex Words* are "real and valuable," Empson remains "the prisoner of his school and decade," playing "the old Cambridge parlour-game, known as the Meaning of Meaning."

J24 Brownjohn, Alan. Review of *Collected Poems*. *Departure* 3 (Spring, 1956), p. 21.

J25 Corke, Hilary. "Riding a Hare." Review of *Collected Poems*. *Listener* 54 (October 6, 1955), p. 565.

Finds "certain astonishing successes amongst these poems" but does not identify them.

J26 Gunn, Thom. Review of *Collected Poems*. *The London Magazine* 3 (February, 1956), pp. 70-75.

Compares the incoherence he finds in Empson's poetry to that he finds in Dylan Thomas's. Names five problems in Empson's verse: "muddled imagery, difficulty of reference, an excessive telescoping of statement, unclearness of tone, and some very odd ways with scansion." Cites "Notes on Local Flora" as one of Empson's best poems, but puzzles over the last line. (See L13 and L26.)

J27 Hartley, Anthony. "Empson and Auden." Review of *Collected Poems*. *Spectator* 195 (December 9, 1955), pp. 815-6.

Recalls the "relief" he felt in reading Empson's poems after WWII: "In short, Mr. Empson appeared as the revenge of the human reason at a moment when many intellectuals (and especially those concerned with the arts) were giving way to a pervasive failure of nerve ranging from a cult of Jungian psychology to a gloomy religiosity that deplored the vulgarity of modern life and an undignified outbreak of happiness among the working classes." Although Empson has a "handful of first-class poems," he is a lesser poet than Auden because "You can't make poetry with a head full of Wittgenstein and a rhyming dictionary."

J28 Hobsbaum, Philip. Review of *Collected Poems*. *Delta* No. 8 (Spring, 1956), pp. 31-7.

Although the latest poems "represent an achievement more distinguished than any poet ... since Eliot," they are very few in number.

J29 Kenner, Hugh. "The Son of Spiders." Review of *Collected Poems*. *Poetry* 76 (April-September, 1950), pp. 150-5.

"The poetry and the criticism alike are the products of a single, disciplined, but 'period', sensibility for which anything may mean anything because nothing has ontological meaning; and endless logical constructions are the sum of all human mental activity."

The components of Empson's world are "Carrolean

nonsense, Eddingtonian quasi-nonsense, logical rigor, witty surprise, social decorum, conversational informality, undergraduate fun and adult seriousness."

J30 Madge, Charles. "Empson Agonistes." Review of *Collected Poems*. *Listen: A Review of Poetry and Criticism* 2 (1956), pp. 19-22.

"The implied statement in the early Empson poems is ... that the relation between the human and the non-human, the poetic and the scientific, the spiritual and the material, the personal and the impersonal, is so subtle that it evaporates in prose but can, in a sense, be expressed in poetry."

J31 Raine, Kathleen. "And Learn a Style from a Despair." Review of *Collected Poems*. *New Statesman* 50 (November 5, 1955), pp. 580-2.

Stresses the importance in Empson's poems of the new ideas in science all around him, and finds that Empson's poetry--like Donne's--reflects a "need for a new imaginative synthesis of knowledge." Asserts that Empson was a deeply "engaged" man who "remains well to the left" of the Oxford poets of his time. "It is only after many readings that we detect, within the Empsonian understatement, more compacted wisdom in two lines, under the brilliant 'metaphysical' trickwork that makes up the complex surface-tensions of this noble poetry, than most of his contemporaries can reach in a thousand."

J32 Rodway, A.E. "The Structure of Complex Verse." Review of *Collected Poems*. *Essays in Criticism* 6 (1956), pp. 232-40.

Makes an important observation about the complexity of Empson's verse: "it is often apparent that ambiguities have been *added* into the poem--like chemicals into a crucible--to make the mixture denser. They have not *grown* as the natural expression of a human experience. Hence the poems in question are complex rather than rich--and the complexity is self-defeating." Concludes that prose is a better medium for "intellectual complexities." Praises Empson for being "perhaps the only modern poet to have refused to retreat from, flinch at, posture before, or simply defy, the fact that 'Life involves maintaining oneself between contradictions,'" which "seems to be his chief general theme." Points out that this theme is "frequently and significantly ... embodied in fire images." One of the most perceptive discussions of Empson's poetry. (See G45.)

J33 Singer, Burns. "In Stars or in Ourselves?" *Encounter* 6, 1 (January, 1956), pp. 82-6.

Judges the poems unsatisfactory in general: "they very seldom reach through to the passionate clarity which is the distinguishing feature of a major poet."

J34 Troy, William. "Poetry and the Non-Euclidean Predicament." Review of *Collected Poems. Poetry* 74 (July, 1949), pp. 234-6.

A "difficult but rewarding volume"--difficult because of the "reference to fields of knowledge and discourse which have rarely and perhaps never with the same degree of intensity been introduced into poetry."

J35 Alvarez, Alfred. "Empson's God." Review of *Milton's God. New Statesman* 62 (September 29, 1961), pp. 442-3.

Says that this book is Empson "airing his quarrel with God." Calls *Milton's God* a "work of obsession," and declares that "if Empson doesn't really believe in God there seems no point in so passionately heaping Him with blame."

J36 Bayley, John. Review of *Milton's God. Spectator* (July 30, 1965), pp. 154-5.

Regrets that Empson "never quite admits that political issues are what he is writing about." Thinks that Empson tends to see ambiguity as "an arrangement of counters simple in themselves."

J37 Brett, R.L. Review of *Milton's God. Critical Quarterly* 3 (1961), pp. 285-7.

Defends the traditional view of *Paradise Lost*, in which Milton is trying to expound Christian doctrines in the face of difficulties raised by his use of the Homeric epic as model.

J38 Broadbent, John. "Myth and Moral." Review of *Milton's God. Time and Tide* 42 (September 21, 1961), p. 1572.

Concludes that "to sketch a critique of Christianity in terms of *Paradise Lost* dulls both."

J39 Daiches, David. "Justifying the Devil." Review of *Milton's God. Spectator* (September 29, 1961), pp. 434-5.

Calls Empson's argument "far-fetched," but judges *Milton's God* "a serious and sparkling book."

J40 Gardner, Helen. "Empson's Milton." Review of *Milton's God. Listener* 66 (October 5, 1961), pp. 521-2.

Despite a generally favorable review, Gardner discerns a flaw in Empson's emphasis on Milton's belief in the Atonement, for he thus overlooks the doctrines that meant most to Milton and shaped *Paradise Lost*: "the doctrine of Creation, the doctrine of Providence, and the belief that the root of all goodness is freedom."

J41 Heath-Stubbs, John. "Tantum Religio...." Review of *Milton's God. X: A Quarterly Review* 2 (1962), pp. 209-11.

Admits that Empson's attack on Christianity "takes its rise from a fundamental human decency and detestation of cruelty and intolerance," but argues that as for the burning of heretics, "It seems at least as likely that the corruption of power, and the perennial desire of the human herd to enforce conformity to itself were as responsible for these enormities as any metaphysical conception."

J42 Hobsbaum, Philip. Review of *Milton's God*. *Listener* 74 (1965), pp. 388-9.

"Professor Empson's interpretation seems to me substantially right, but I cannot see in what way it makes the poem any better."

J43 Kenner, Hugh. "The Critic's Not for Burning." Review of *Milton's God*. *National Review* 13, 8 (August, 1962), pp. 149-51.

Replies sarcastically to Empson's polemic against Christianity: "He is the period piece he always was, an anxious nineteenth-century liberal who got it into his head at an early age that what they told you in church was cramping, not to say nasty."

J44 Parker, William Riley. "Paradox Lost." Review of *Milton's God*. *Virginia Quarterly Review* 38 (1962), pp. 332-5.

Dismisses *Milton's God*, which is "misleading as the devil." Points to Empson's misquotations from other critics, and cites two previous sources for the thesis of Empson's chapter on Delilah.

J45 Ricks, Christopher. Review of *Milton's God*. *New Statesman* (August 27, 1965), pp. 292-3.

Notes the failure of the first edition of *Milton's God* to make any impact on scholarship, and observes that "The magic word for making the whole argument vanish has been *'donnée'*...." Remarks apropos of the destruction of the Philistines in *Samson Agonistes*, "There are limits to what a *donnée* in great literature can be asked to digest, and genocide is beyond them." Asserts further that God's justice is the subject of *Paradise Lost*, not the *donnée*, and that Milton was not afraid to argue about his God. Disagrees with Empson on one point: "although Milton may well have been attracted *unconsciously* to a criticism of God, this is very different from arguing that Milton *consciously* doubted that God was just."

J46 Robson, W.W. "More Empson than Milton?" Review of *Milton's God*. *The Oxford Review* (1966), pp. 1928-35.

Finds *Milton's God* a welcome corrective to the "eccentric" views of C.S. Lewis and E.M.W. Tillyard; approves the "campaign against the critics for whom 'humanist' and 'liberal' are words of abuse"; but concludes (1) that as an attack on Christianity *Milton's God* is "confused and inconsequent"; (2) that Empson discerns "human fineness" in Milton "where it is not"; (3) that "Empson's own work ... is a more convincing demonstration that it is possible for a mind to be subtle and devious, yet kind and honest"; and (4) that even though his "interpretations and commentaries often bring out an extra sparkle and vivacity in the great poem," Empson's book "does not remove the incoherences in *Paradise Lost*, but increases one's sense of them." (See G72.)

J46a Robson, W.W. "Mr. Empson on *Paradise Lost*. *Critical Essays*. London: Routledge and Kegan Paul, 1966. Pp. 87-98.

Reprint of J46.

J47 Steadman, John. Review of *Milton's God*. *Archiv* 200 (1963), pp. 299-301.

Calls *Milton's God* "an interesting and entertaining failure."

J48 Anonymous. Review of *Coleridge's Verse: A Selection*. *TLS* (December 15, 1972), p. 1524.

Rejects Empson's interpretation of "The Ancient Mariner" as an adventure story about the maritime trade.

K

REVIEWS OF BOOKS ABOUT EMPSON

K1 Fuller, Roy. "Too High-Flown a Genius?" Review of Gardner (H2) and Norris (H6). *Encounter* 53 (July, 1979), pp. 41-8.

Gives high praise to *The God Approached* (H2), an "indispensable" book that "opens up the whole of the verse for evaluation." Identifies some jarring "prosodic lapses" in Empson's verse, and agrees that some of Empson's poetry is infected with what Ian Hamilton describes as a "lethal silliness."

Norris's book (H6) is marred by "the disfiguring birthmarks of the thesis."

K2 Sale, Roger. "The Sustenance of Reason." Review of Gardner (H2) and Norris (H6). *TLS* (December 1, 1978), pp. 1382-3.

Praises the Gardners' book (H2) as an "excellent guide." Disparages Norris's book (H6) for its pursuit of philosophy, which Sale thinks is not the point of Empson's criticism.

K3 Donoghue, Denis. "Trusting to Language and Common Sense." Review of Gardner (H2) and Norris (H6). *Times Higher Education Supplement* (October 20, 1978), p. 15.

On Norris (H6): his portrait of Empson is "a little too hearty to be true." Empson's mind, Donoghue says, "works harder and moves faster than that of any other modern critic," and makes him hard to reconcile with Norris's "bluff, hale and hearty figure."

Judges the Gardners' explications "generally excellent." Their book is "invaluable for clearing up "all kinds of darkness in the poems." Includes a fine photograph of Empson.

K4 Donoghue, Denis. Review of Gill (H3). *TLS* (June 7, 1974), pp. 597-8.

Observes that in Empson's short reviews, "brevity is often the soul of truculence." Wonders why Karl Miller "conspired with Empson to elicit the most tedious part of the reviewer's mind, his hatred of Christianity." Claims that Empson's "grandeur of spirit" becomes "pinched and nasty" in dealing with Christianity. Calls *Some Versions of Pastoral* Empson's masterpiece--it does not "supply a method but classic examples of a mind's pliancy exercised in the best of causes."

K5 Fuller, John. "An Edifice of Meaning: On William Empson." Review of Gill (H3). *Encounter* (November, 1974), pp. 75-9.

Declares that "Empson is in fact a poet of vision, where the only true vision is a question of discovering what man's position in the world really is." Devotes most of his review to a discussion of Christopher Ricks's "showpiece" essay (see I84) and compares Empson's poetic devices to Dylan Thomas's: "the straits that Empson sometimes gets into result from the attempt to maintain a polymetaphorical structure, a storeyed edifice of meaning, whereas Thomas indulges in linear association backwards and forwards, the couplings of a shunted train." Provides an alternative explication of "Invitation to Juno," an example of "argufying."

K6 Norris, Christopher. Review of Gill (H3). *Critical Quarterly* 18, 4 (1976), pp. 90-96.

Finds something "myopic and self-willed" in the Ricks essay; admires Hough's piece (see I51) as "a useful discussion of an ultimate problem in literary theory"; speculates that "it was the peculiar, even compromised nature of his current critical involvement which caused the falling-off in Empson's poetic output during the years of preparation for *Complex Words*"; and points out "how Empson's own style, with its flat, colloquial yet analytical character, is often the audible result of 'putting it into Basic' or something very like it."

"The only collective fault of these essays is that they tend to underrate, by failing in themselves to meet, the tough, recalcitrant rationalism of Empson's makeup."

K7 Ogawa, Kazuo. "Empson Taishoku Kinen Essay-shu." *Eigo Seinen* (Tokyo) 120 (1974), pp. 356-8.

Review of Gill (H3).

K8 Paschall, Douglas. Review of Gill (H3). *Sewanee Review* 83 (1975), pp. xlvi-li.

Praises the essays by Hough and Ricks, but feels that Ricks "overstates the case by making the idea of 'begetting' greatly *more* 'daunting and exhilirating' than it is."

K9 Wood, Michael. "Incomparable Empson." Review of Gill (H3). *New York Review of Books* (January 23, 1975), pp. 30-33.

Takes care of the Gill *Festschrift* in a hurry ("It is all a bit too amiable and soft on the edges") and takes the four critical books in order. *Seven Types* is a "mischievous book ... which delights in multiplying complicated meanings" and provides the most "sheer pleasure" of Empson's works. The essays on Alice (in A2), on *King Lear* (in A3), and on *Tom Jones* (D55) are indeed Empson's most dazzling pieces. *Milton's God* is a "brilliant business" that "just seems freighted with a load of cares and emotions which probably belong in another kind of book altogether." *Complex Words* is "slightly hindered by his rejection of large theories" and "can seem downright plodding in comparison with his flighty French contemporaries."

K10 Berhart, Walter. Review of Meller (H4). *Germanisch-romanische Monatsschrift* (Heidelberg) 28 (1978), pp. 254-7.

K11 Beaver, Harold. "Tilting at Windbags." Review of Norris (H6). *New Statesman* 96 (August 11, 1978), pp. 185-6.

Sketches lucidly Empson's place in modern criticism: "he plays Sancho Panza tilting at the quixotic windbags of Eng. Lit." Despite his attacks on the Intentional Fallacy, intentionality is still, "arguably, Empson's weakest link." Norris's book shows a very exact awareness of the 20th-century Anglo-American tradition in which Empson has played his creative and maverick role."

K12 Cain, William. "Marveling at Empson's Ways." Review of Norris (H6). *Virginia Quarterly Review* 55 (Summer, 1979), pp. 540-45.

Observes that recent critics (e.g., Culler, Bloom) refer admiringly to Empson's work, but points out that Empson has always been considered "brilliant and influential." Empson remains difficult to assess, however. His style is often oblique, some find his scholarship inadequate, and his characteristic fairness is clouded by the severity of his anti-Christian polemics. On balance, Empson's work is "rich and rewarding" and he deserves praise for his "spirit of rational inquiry."

K13 Hill, Geoffrey. Review of *The Review* (special Empson number: see H7). *Essays in Criticism* 14 (1964), pp. 91-101.

Most of the essay is devoted to discussion of various Empson poems.

K14 Anonymous. Review of Sale (H8). *TLS* (July 27, 1973), p. 848.

Finds nothing of value in Sale's book.

K15 Pritchard, William. Review of Sale (H8). *Modern Language Quarterly* 35 (1974), pp. 92-5.

Describes the chapter on Empson as "difficult, brilliantly alive" and claims that it constitutes "the most astute account of the English literary-critical scene, 1925 and beyond, encountered in some time."

K16 Ricks, Christopher. "Prophets." Review of Sale (H8). *New York Review of Books* (January 24, 1974), pp. 43-6.

Not persuaded that Empson belongs with "the tragic deplorers of the modern world." Thinks that Sale's approach produces a "saddening disparagement" of *Complex Words*.

K17 Russo, John Paul. Review of Sale (H8). *Modern Philology* 73 (1975), pp. 100-104.

Judges Sale's study "among the very best criticism to date" on Empson's development. Disagrees with Sale's view that Empson's major work is "done" by the time he gets to *Milton's God*.

K18 Stoker, Richard J. Review of Sale (H8). *Modern Fiction Studies* 19 (1973), pp. 636-8.

"The writing on Empson ... takes too many pains to present a theory that is old hat: the 'community' of critic, reader, and author."

L

MISCELLANEOUS

L1 Anonymous. Letter. *TLS* (October 12, 1973), p. 1234.

This is the *TLS* reviewer's answer to G91.

L2 Auden, W.H. "A Toast (To Professor William Empson on the occasion of his retirement in 1971)." In *William Empson: The Man and His Work*, ed. Roma Gill. London and Boston: Routledge and Kegan Paul, 1974. P. 1.

"Our verbal games are separate, thank heaven ...."

L3 Bell, Julian. "The Progress of Poetry: A Letter to a Contemporary." *Cambridge Review* (March 7, 1930).

A brief reminiscence.

L4 Berry, Francis. "William Empson." In *William Empson: The Man and His Work*, ed. Roma Gill. London and Boston: Routledge and Kegan Paul, 1974. Pp. 208-12.

A poetical tribute. Sample:

> Witty and lucky and plucky this man,
> He came as a legend, he left as a myth
> At the bars, by our fires, with his verse, with his prose,
> His extraordinary dares, his amazingly wise--
> Or his occasionally wild, quite lunatick--flairs
>
> He left with even more lustre than he began.

L5 Bottrall, Ronald. "William Empson." In *William Empson: The Man and His Work*, ed. Roma Gill. London and Boston: Routledge and Kegan Paul, 1974. Pp. 49-51.

A poem about "A genial man, perhaps a genius."

L6 Brooks, Cleanth. "Postscript." *Sewanee Review* 55 (October, 1955), pp. 697-9.

Disarming response to D30, explaining that he treated certain minor poems to demonstrate that "they too participate in the principles which organize Donne's 'Canonization' and Shakespeare's *Macbeth*."

L7 Brownjohn, Alan. "William Empson at Aldermaston." *The Railings*. London: The Digby Press, 1961.

A poem in seventeen quatrains.

L7a Brownjohn, Alan. "William Empson at Aldermaston." *Penguin Modern Poets 14*. Harmondsworth and Baltimore: Penguin, 1969. Pp. 20-22.

Reprint of L7.

L8 Calinescu, Matei. "William Empson." *Gazeta literara* (România) 39 (1968), p. 8.

L9 Fraser, George. Letter. *Critical Quarterly* 1 (Winter, 1959), pp. 352-3.

Criticizes Empson for his remarks about Christians as "loathsome torture-worshipers."

L10 Gardner, Helen. "John Donne." *Critical Quarterly* 8 (1966), pp. 374-7.

Answer to D75. Elaborates on her procedures in editing Donne's poems. (See also L21.)

L11 Graves, Robert. Letter. *Modern Language Quarterly* 27 (1966), pp. 255-6.

Answers Jensen's essay (see I54) with the admission that he's never read *Seven Types*: "the use of the word 'ambiguity' to express rather the *congruity* of combined poetic meanings put me off."

L12 Grigson, Geoffrey. Letter. *Poetry* 50 (May, 1937), pp. 115-6.

Attacks Empson nastily, calling his work "quarter-man stuff so unreadably trivial that it is not worth insulting or attacking." (See D23, G28, G29.)

L13 Gunn, Thom. Letter. *The London Magazine* 3 (April, 1956), pp. 64-5.

Questions Kathleen Raine's "ruling that the whole field of knowledge to which a poet may refer 'should be the whole body of knowledge of his society.'" (See J26 and L26.)

L14 Hume. Robert D. "Dryden's Apparent Scepticism." *Essays in Criticism* 20 (1970), pp. 492-5.

A response to D83: "Dryden is neither philosopher nor saint, and indeed he could be a bit of a twister, but I think his religious professions deserve more serious sympathy and consideration than Mr. Empson allows them."

L15 Jensen, James. Letter. *Modern Language Quarterly* 27 (1966), pp. 258-9.

Replies to L11 and G71.

L16 Kell, Richard. "Empsonium." *The London Magazine* 6 (October, 1959), pp. 55-6.

Poem with notes, in the style of Empson.

L17 Lanning, George. "Memories of the School of English." In *John Crowe Ransom: Gentleman, Teacher, Poet, Editor, Founder of 'The Kenyon Review.' A Tribute from the Community of Letters*, ed. D. David Long and Michael R. Burr. Supplement to *The Kenyon Collegian* 90, 7 (1964), pp, 33-5.

Recalls Empson as an enthusiastic baseball player, "running for base, beard blowing over one shoulder, and daisies in the long grass under his feet." Also explains Empson's fondness for murder mysteries: "he read them, he told me, to see if he could guess the copyright date from internal evidence."

L18 Lewis, C.S. "'Ingenium' and Wit." *Studies in Words*. Cambridge: Cambridge University Press, 1967. Pp. 90-96.

Argues against Empson's claim in D38 that in Pope's "Essay on Criticism" there is always a joke associated with the word "wit."

L19 Maxwell, J.C. Letter. *Essays in Criticism* 17 (1967), pp. 257-8.

In the Shakespeare Folio the spelling is 'barstadie,' not 'barstardy.' Says he's never heard a distinction in pronunciation. (See L20, D77, and D79.)

L20 Maxwell, J.C. Letter. *Essays in Criticism* 18 (1968), p. 112.

Continues the dispute started in L19. (See D77 and D79.)

L21 Merchant, W.P.H. Letter. *Critical Quarterly* 8 (1966), pp. 377-80.

Comments on Empson's review of Gardner's edition of Donne (see D75), defending Gardner's method (see L10) and criticizes Empson for violating "almost every rule of textual criticism."

L22 Miner, Earl. "Dryden's Apparent Scepticism." *Essays in Criticism* 21 (1971), pp. 410-11.

Finds Empson's argument in D83 "creative," remarking that "he confuses the mental processes of Milton and Dryden with his own."

L23 Nelson, John O. "An Essay (in Notes and Verses) on the Question Whether Individual Words in a Poem Have One Meaning or Several Meanings." In *Language and Aesthetics*, ed. Benjamin R. Tilghman. Lawrence: University Press of Kansas, 1973. Pp. 155-62.

Just what the title says. A sample:

> "Is the word's meaning many or is it one?
> Is Kittredge right, or Empson right, or none?"

L24 Parsons, J.M. "T.S. Eliot's Critical Reputation." *Critical Quarterly* 8 (1966), pp. 180-81.

Letter in response to George Watson's essay (see L33) on Eliot and the question of who influenced whom in *New Bearings* and *Seven Types*.

L25 Purcell, James M. "Lewis on Empson: Was Eden Plato's or OGPU's?" *Bulletin of the New York C.S. Lewis Society* 4, 6 (1973), pp. 6-8.

Summarizes the differences between Empson and Lewis as interpreters of *Paradise Lost*.

L26 Raine, Kathleen. Letter. *The London Magazine* 3 (March, 1956), pp. 66-7.

Defends Empson against Thom Gunn (see J26), claiming that Empson "has asked of his readers no more than poets of other times." Explains the allusions to trees in "Note on Local Flora."

L27 Richards, I.A. Letter. *Modern Language Quarterly* 27 (September, 1966), p. 255.

Answers Jensen's essay (see I54) about the gestation of *Seven Types*: "This seems to me not *bad* fiction and I've no wish to offer any rival account."

L28 Ricks, Christopher. "William Empson in Conversation with Christopher Ricks." *The Review: A Magazine of Poetry and Criticism* (June, 1963), pp. 26-35.

Annotated at G63.

L29 Sale, Roger. Letter. *Hudson Review* 20 (1967), p. 538.

Note in reply to G79.

L30 Salgado, Gamini. "The Argument about Shakespeare's Characters." *Critical Quarterly* 7 (Winter, 1965), p. 384.

For the background of this essay, see G68 and M36.

L31 Sissman, L.E. "Just a Whack at Empson." *The Review: A Magazine of Poetry and Criticism* (June, 1963), p. 75.

A poem. See E46.

L32 Sparrow, John. Answer to "O Miselle Passer!" *Oxford Outlook* 10 (1930), pp. 598-607.

Answer to D5. (See M52.)

L33 Watson, George. "The Triumph of T.S. Eliot." *Critical Quarterly* 7 (Winter, 1965-66).

Raises the question of who influenced whom in *New Bearings* and *Seven Types*. (See L24.)

L34 Watson, George. Letter. *Critical Quarterly* 8 (1966), pp. 181-2.

Response to L24.

L35 Wren-Lewis, John. Letter. *Critical Quarterly* 6 (1964), p. 84.

See G64 and G65.

M

BACKGROUND

M1 Barfield, Owen. *Poetic Diction: A Study in Meaning*. London: Faber and Gwyer, 1928. 216 pp.

Empson discusses this "excellent book" in A3.

M2 Beardsley, Monroe. *Aesthetics: Problems in the Philosophy of Criticism*. New York: Harcourt, Brace and Company, 1958. 614 pp.

Contents: I. Aesthetic Objects; II. The Categories of Critical Analysis; III. The Literary Work; IV. Artistic Form; V. Form in Literature; VI. Representation in the Visual Arts. VII. The Meaning of Music. VIII. Artistic Truth. IX. Literature and Knowledge. X. Critical Evaluation. XI. Aesthetic Value. XII. The Arts in the Life of Man.

Much of this broad survey is given over to annotation of the many pertinent works cited. Sympathetic allusions to Empson are commonly embedded in these succinct bibliographical surveys.

M3 Bennett, Joan. "God, Satan, and King Charles: Milton's Royal Portraits." *PMLA* 92 (1977), pp. 441-57.

Argues that there is considerable parallelism between the monarchy of Charles I in Milton's prose works and the tyranny of Satan in *Paradise Lost*. Thus, the prose works constitute a useful gloss on the poem. (See G97.)

M4 Bennett, Joan. "Milton's God." *PMLA* 93 (1978), pp. 119-20.

Answers Empson's letter in G97. "Milton wanted our response ultimately to include an intellectual understanding of the cause for our contradictory *feelings* and a moral analysis and judgment of them."

M5 Bentley, Richard, ed. *Milton's "Paradise Lost." A New Edition*. London, 1732.

This work, discussed by Empson in A2, is usefully reprinted in the following:

"Bentley's emendations to *Paradise Lost*." In *Milton, 1732-1801: The Critical Heritage*, ed. John T. Shawcross. London and Boston: Routledge and Kegan Paul, 1972. Pp. 41-50.

M6 Bloomfield, Leonard. *Language*. New York: Henry Holt, 1933. 564 pp.

See Empson's objections to this book in A3, pp. 434-43.

M7 Booth, Stephen. *An Essay on Shakespeare's Sonnets*. New Haven and London: Yale University Press, 1969. Pp. 152-68.

Assesses Empson's reading of Shakespeare's Sonnet 94 in A2, comparing it with other modern interpretations.

M8 Bradley, A.C. *Shakespearean Tragedy*. London: Macmillan, 1904. 498 pp.

Discussed by Empson in his essay on *King Lear* (D34): "I must try to give a summary of Bradley's position about the gods, as it has the great merit of exploring the alternatives."

M9 Brooks, Cleanth, and Robert Penn Warren. "Ambiguity, Added Dimension, and Submerged Metaphor." *Understanding Poetry: An Anthology for College Students*, rev. ed. New York: Henry Holt, 1950. Pp. 571-89.

"A better term for poetic ambiguity is *richness*."

M10 Caudwell, Christopher. *Illusion and Reality: A Study of the Sources of Poetry*. New York: International Publishers, 1937. 342 pp.

In a murky account of "poetic irrationality," a Marxist verdict on ambiguity is given: "This ambiguity, which Empson takes to be the essence of poetry, is in fact a by-product." (See p. 204.)

M11 Chatman, Seymour, and Samuel R. Levin, ed. *Essays on the Language of Literature*. Boston: Houghton Mifflin Company, 1967. 450 pp.

Contents: I. Sound Texture; II. Metrics; III. Grammar; IV. Literary Form and Meaning; V. Style and Stylistics.

Useful essays for students of Empson to consult.

M12 Collinge, N.E. "Ambiguity in Literature: Some Guidelines." *Arethusa* 2 (1969), pp. 13-29.

Offers principles of identifying examples of ambiguity, using examples from classical literature.

M13 Elton, William. *A Glossary of the New Criticism*. Chicago: Modern Poetry Association, 1949. 48 pp.

Helpful definitions and discussions of the terms used by the New Critics. A shorter version was published in the December, 1948, and February, 1949, issues of *Poetry*.

M14 Graves, Robert, and Riding, Laura. *A Survey of Modernist Poetry*. London: William Heinemann, 1927.

See annotation under Riding, Laura (M47).

M15 Gray, Bennison. *The Phenomenon of Literature*. The Hague and Paris: Mouton, 1975. 594 pp.

This long study argues for the notion of literature as fiction, not language. The references to Empson are contemptuous of his "far-fetched interpretations."

M16 Grubb, Frederick. *A Vision of Reality: A Study of Liberalism in Twentieth-Century Verse.* London: 1965. Pp. 128-34.

"Empson's genial reserve is now seen to be a delayed-action tactic for the realization of something immensely significant: for Empson embodies a poetic acclimatization of liberal empiricism in a manner vital to the debate about the two Cultures; in fact, Empson, of whom C.P. Snow never appears to have heard, has anticipated and solved many of his cherished worries."

M17 Hirsch, E.D., Jr. *Validity in Interpretation.* New Haven and London: Yale University Press, 1967. 287 pp.

Well known modern defense of the objective text, pointing to *Seven Types* as a heretical work that "demonstrates on almost every page what happens to interpretation when a text is self-consciously conceived to be a 'piece of language,' and the problem of validity is ignored."

M18 Hobsbaum, Philip. "The Growth of English Modernism." *Wisconsin Studies in Contemporary Literature* 6 (1965), pp. 97-105.

Empson is described as the most interesting of a group of "unjustly neglected" poets of the thirties.

M19 Jackson, Laura (Riding). "Some Autobiographical Corrections of Literary History." *Denver Quarterly* 8 (1974), pp. 1-33.

Gives in pp. 12-14 her view of the relationship between *Seven Types* and *A Survey of Modernist Poetry*. Speaking of the wrongs she feels were done her in reference to her part in the authorship of the *Survey* with Robert Graves: "Not to be omitted are not rare absences entire of my name, where the collaboratively presented thought, attitudes, judgements, are found critically considered. In my personal tracking-down of cases of behavior of the second class, to their authors, I have met with very pleasant apologies, and a few sober awakenings to answerableness for serious remissness. Only one of the public deniers to me of due credits and amenities has in private address to me defended the denial--the defence being, I should append, of the nature of an offensive. This was a person who had more reason than any other, except one (Mr. Graves), for personal gratitude for what I put into the Survey: it was Mr. Empson." (See I54, L11, M47, and G71.)

M20 Johnson, Michael. "William Empson: A Chronological Bibliography." *Bulletin of Bibliography* 29, 4 (1973), pp. 134-9.

Takes the Empson bibliography to 1970, with the exception of some of the earlier pieces, notably the *Granta* reviews.

M21 Johnson, William C. *Milton Criticism: A Subject Index*. Folkestone: Dawson, 1978. 450 pp.

Convenient source of references to Empson by Milton scholars.

M22 Kazin, Alfred. *On Native Grounds*. New York: Reynal and Hitchcock, 1942. Pp. 444-5.

In a brief section heavy with contempt for the "lay scientists of letters," Kazin dismisses Empson as one of those "field scientists of metaphor" who "promised a substitute for the loose chitchat of nonscientific minds," and who "raised the professional prestige of criticism at the expense of every human need of literature as prophecy or history or sustenance."

M23 Krieger, Murray. *The New Apologists for Poetry*.

Only brief references to Empson, but an important study of the theories of the New Critics that students of *Seven Types* would probably want to read.

M24 Lee, Brian. "The New Criticism and the Language of Poetry." In *Essays on Style and Language*, ed. Roger Fowler. London: Routledge and Kegan Paul, 1966. Pp. 29-52.

Brief mention of Empson in a survey of the tenets of the New Critics.

M25 Lowbridge, Peter. "An Empson Bibliography." *The Review: A Magazine of Poetry and Criticism* (June, 1963), pp. 63-74.

"The Bibliography attempts to cover all the published works, and carries selected correspondence, up to April, 1963, with the following exceptions: very early contributions, consisting of reviews of films, books and magazines, and miscellaneous writings, including verse parodies, to the Cambridge magazine *Granta* (Vols. 36-8, 1926-29), re-prints of poems in later anthologies; unrevised reprints of critical articles."

M26 Megaw, Moira. "An Empson Bibliography." In *William Empson: The Man and His Work*, ed. Roma Gill. London and Boston: Routledge and Kegan Paul, 1974. Pp. 213-44.

Exceptionally useful. Includes everything of consequence through 1972.

M27 Merrill, Thomas. "'The Sacrifice' and the Structure of Religious Language." *Language and Style* (Autumn, 1969), pp. 275-87.

Argues for the unique structure of religious language, bringing up Empson only to cast him aside: "Empson understands the task of 'The Sacrifice' to state a generalized solution of the conflicts inherent in Christian theology, but the aim of religious language is precisely the opposite of this." (See A1, D40, F78, and M62a.)

M28 Miles, Josephine. "More Semantics of Poetry." *Kenyon Review* 2 (1940), pp. 502-7.

Objects to Wheelwright's basic distinction in M63 between the monosign and the plurisign, finding poetic language to be "a specialization of language by intensities through the forms and patterns of the verse line." Calls for more empirical study of "poetic content." All usage is plurisignative, but certain meanings are played down in one context, played up in another; and "poetry wishes to press ... those meanings richest and fullest in the thought of its own time."

M28a Miles, Josephine. "More Semantics of Poetry." In *Essays on the Language of Literature*, ed. Seymour Chatman and Samuel R. Levin. Boston: Houghton Mifflin Company, 1967. Pp. 264-8.

Reprint of M28.

M29 Morris, Charles. *Signs, Language and Behavior*. New York: Prentice-Hall, 1946. 365 pp.

Empson discusses this book in A3, pp. 429-34: "He starts much further back than I do, and never reaches the kind of case I want to handle...."

M30 Muller, Herbert. "The New Criticism in Poetry." *Southern Review* 6 (Spring, 1941), pp. 811-39.

Only minor references to Empson, but a good background essay.

M31 Murray, Patrick. *Milton: The Modern Phase. A Study of Twentieth-Century Criticism*. New York: Barnes and Noble, 1967. Pp. 75-6.

Summarizes the controversy over the accusation that Milton had inserted into the *Eikon Basilike* a prayer that he had attacked in *Eikonoklastes*; also provides bibliographical notes (pp. 145-6). (See A4b.)

M32 Needham, John. *"The Completest Mode": I. A. Richards and the Continuity of English Criticism*. Edinburgh: Edinburgh University Press, 1982.

Analyzes (in "A critique of Empson," pp. 3-10) the types of ambiguity and finds that Empson shares a "community of spirit" with Samuel Johnson.

M33 Nicholson, Marjorie Hope. *John Milton: A Reader's Guide to His Poetry*. New York: Octagon Books, 1971.

Summarizes briefly Empson's remarks on Delilah, placing his commentary in a context of general discussion by others such as Hansford and Tillyard.

M34 Noble, Yvonne. *John Gay, "The Beggar's Opera": A Critical Edition*. Yale University Dissertation, 1966. 400 pp.

Acknowledges a debt to Empson "throughout the critique and the critical annotation of this edition." Calls Empson's essay (D13) on *The Beggar's Opera* "brilliant, provocative, and exasperating."

M35 Norris, Christopher. "Derrida at Yale: The 'Deconstructive Moment' in Modernist Poetics." *Philosophy and Literature* 4 (Fall, 1980), pp. 242-56.

This account of Derrida's differences with the New Critics credits Empson with having "opened up the literary text to a practice of reading which released as many ambiguities, overtones, and hints of recondite meaning as the analyst could *reasonably* claim to find in it," and sees Empson as doing "a species of 'deconstructive' criticism" in his treatment of Wordsworth and Fielding. Empson spurned the New Critics' dogmas of the Intentional Fallacy and the Verbal Icon, retaining the author as the source of meaning and so drawing back from the maze of deconstructive play.

M36 Nuttall, A.D. "The Argument about Shakespeare's Characters." *Critical Quarterly* 7 (Summer, 1965), pp. 107-20.

Empson inserted himself into this argument in G68. (See also L30.)

M37 O'Connor, William Van. "Analytical Criticism." *An Age of Criticism: 1900-1950*. Chicago: Henry Regnery Company, 1952. Pp. 156-75.

Surveys the New Critics, crediting Empson with "demonstrating that language tends to be highly connotative."

M38 Ogden, C.K., and I.A. Richards. *The Meaning of Meaning: A Study of the Influence of Language upon Thought and of the Science of Symbolism*. London: Kegan Paul, Trench, Trubner; New York: Harcourt, Brace, 1923.

Important background work on aspects of language (e.g., its Emotive and Cognitive qualities) of interest to Empson. (See A3, p. 11.)

M39 Peter, John. *A Critique of "Paradise Lost."* New York: Columbia University Press; London: Longmans, 1960.

An excellent study, of which Empson says, "I am much in sympathy with his book" (A4, p. 41).

M40 Peter, John. "Lady Chatterley for the Last Time." *Essays in Criticism* (July, 1963), pp. 301-3.

See Empson's contribution to this discussion in D64.

M41 Peyre, Henri. *Writers and Their Critics: A Study of Misunderstanding.* Ithaca: Cornell University Press, 1944.

Sharply sceptical of the whole undertaking of criticism ("There have been fortunate ages in which critics were an unborn or rare species"), especially of the "veritable epidemic of criticism" in America. Empson and Richards are described as "arid and austere mountains" giving birth to "infinitesimal mice." A collection of disgruntlements.

M41a Peyre, Henri. *The Failures of Criticism.* Ithaca: Cornell University Press, 1967.

Emended edition of M41.

M42 Raine, Kathleen. "Extracts from Unpublished Memoirs." In *William Empson: The Man and His Work*, ed. Roma Gill. London and Boston: Routledge and Kegan Paul, 1974. Pp. 13-20.

Engrossing memoir of the author's friendship with Empson when they were contemporaries at Cambridge and she was submitting poems to *Experiment*.

M42a Raine, Kathleen. *The Land Unknown.* New York: George Braziller, 1975.

Chapter Two is a revised version of M42.

M43 Richards, I.A. "Cambridge Poetry." *Granta* 38 (March 8, 1929), p. 359.

M44 Richards, I.A. *Science and Poetry*. New York: W.W. Norton, 1926.

Classic statement of the place of poetry in a world where "the average educated man is growing more conscious." The poetic experience puts the competing attractions and distractions of life "back into equilibrium." The sound and feel of words are primary in poetry, their sense secondary. "Most words are ambiguous as regards their plain sense; especially in poetry. We can take them as we please in a variety of senses." The passing of the Magical View of the world poses a problem for poetry, which proceeds by scientifically unverifiable "pseudostatement." The loss of many large pseudostatements about God and the Universe has left man in a crisis: "Over whole tracts of natural emotional response we are to-day like a bed of dahlias whose sticks have been removed." We must face up to the truth that "experience is its own justification" even though "we still hunger after a basis in belief." It is, presumably, the value of great poetry that it enables us to put this experience into satisfying order. Empson says (D42, pp. 131-2), "The main theme of *Science and Poetry* ... is that the arts, especially poetry, can save the world from the disasters which will otherwise follow the general loss of religious and semi-religious belief."

M44a Richards, I.A. "How Does a Poem Know When It Is Finished?" *Poetries and Sciences*. London: Routledge and Kegan Paul, 1970.

This essay is part of the commentary (pp. 85-121) added in the reissue of M44.

M45 Richards, I.A. "William Empson." *Furioso* 1 (January 12, 1940). Supplement.

Describes his experience as Empson's Director of Studies at Cambridge. "At about his third visit he brought up the games of interpretation which Laura Riding and Robert Graves had been playing with the unpunctuated form of 'The expense of spirit in a waste of shame.' Taking the sonnet as a conjuror takes his hat, he produced an endless swarm of lively rabbits from it and ended by 'You could do that with any poetry, couldn't you?' This was a Godsend to a Director of Studies, so I said, 'You'd better go off and do it, hadn't you?' A week later he said he was still slapping away at it on his typewriter. Would I mind if he just went on with that? Not a bit. The following week there he was with a thick wad of very illegible typescript under his arm--the central 30,000 words or so of the book." (See M47, I54, M19.)

M46 Ricks, Christopher. *Milton's Grand Style*. Oxford: The Clarendon Press, 1963.

Attempts to "refute Milton's detractors by showing the kind of life there is in the verse of *Paradise Lost*." Refers freely to Empson and observes that "Though the following pages owe everything to Empsonian criticism, they try to slow down the process which in Mr. Empson is so agonizingly nimble."

M47 Riding, Laura, and Robert Graves. *A Survey of Modernist Poetry*. London: William Heinemann, 1927.

The discussion of Shakespeare's 129th sonnet in this book was revealed by I.A. Richards to have been the model for the method of *Seven Types of Ambiguity*. (See M45, I54, and M19.)

M47a Riding, Laura, and Robert Graves. *A Survey of Modernist Poetry*. Edinburgh: The Folcroft Press, 1971.

Reprint of M47.

M48 Schaar, Claes. "Old Texts and Ambiguity." *English Studies* 46 (1965), pp. 157-65.

Finds that Empson's ambiguities of types four, five, six, and seven are all concerned with one kind of psychological factor, and subsumed under type one. Types two and three "are not in the same way bound up with different psychological factors." Thinks that his review of the ambiguities in old texts provides "some support for the belief that ambiguities of the types defined by Prof. Empson perhaps did not loom very large in the attitude to language of these earlier ages."

M49 Smith, Hallett. *Elizabethan Poetry*. Cambridge, Mass.: Harvard University Press, 1952.

Discusses Empson's reading of Shakespeare's Sonnet 94 and argues against him that the doctrine of the octet is "the exact opposite of the argument in the first seventeen sonnets of the cycle."

M49a Smith, Hallett. "Pastoral Poetry: The Vitality and Versatility of a Convention." In *A Mirror for Modern Scholars,* ed. Lester A. Beaurline. New York: Odyssey Press, 1966. Pp. 357-82.

Reprinted from M49.

M50 Smith, James. "The Metaphysical Conceit." *Scrutiny* 2 (1933-34), pp. 222-39.

Important and influential early essay on the metaphysical poets. Calls Herbert, Donne, and Marvell the three major English metaphysical poets.

M51 Smith, Janet. "A Is B at 8,000 Feet." In *William Empson: The Man and His Work,* ed. Roma Gill. London and Boston: Routledge and Kegan Paul, 1974. Pp. 34-40.

Empson and logic in the French Alps.

M52 Sparrow, John. "The New Criticism." *Farrago* (February, 1930), pp. 22-34.

This is the essay criticizing I.A. Richards that Empson replies to in D5. (See also L32.)

M53 Stallman, Robert Wooster. "The New Criticism and the Southern Critics." In *A Southern Vanguard*, ed. Allen Tate. New York: Prentice-Hall, 1947. Pp. 28-51.

This synthesis of the ideas and methods of the New Critics mentions Empson but briefly--a mathematician-poet offers nothing for Stallman's central issue of the dissociation of sensibility--but Empson is cited for the excellence of his technical criticism and for his influence on Brooks.

M53a Stallman, Robert Wooster. "The New Critics." In *Critiques and Essays in Criticism, 1920-1948,* ed. Robert Wooster Stallman. New York: Ronald Press, 1949. Pp. 488-506.

Reprint of M53.

M54 Stallman, Robert Wooster, ed. *Critiques and Essays in Criticism, 1920-1948: Representing the Achievement of Modern British and American Critics.* New York: Ronald Press, 1949.

Valuable anthology of over 500 pages, including a lengthy, rich bibliography as well as important essays.

M55 Stern, Gustaf. *Meaning and Change of Meaning.* Goteborg: Elanders Boktryckeri Aktiebolag, 1931. 456 pp.

Empson begins *The Structure of Complex Words* with a discussion of this book, and there are several other scattered references to it. Empson remarks: "I was made to realize that the Emotive approach could go absurdly wrong through an otherwise excellent treatise ... by Gustaf Stern."

M55a Stern, Gustaf. *Meaning and Change of Meaning.* Bloomington: Indiana University Press, 1965.

Reprint of M55. (Not a translation; the original was in English.)

M56 Stevenson, Charles L. *Ethics and Language.* New Haven: Yale University Press, 1944.

See Empson's discussion in A3, pp. 414-9, of Stevenson's advocacy of the Emotive view of language.

M57 Swan, Jim. "At Play in the Garden of Ambivalence: Andrew Marvell and the Green World." *Criticism* 17 (1975), pp. 295-307.

Concentrates on stanzas V through VII of "The Garden," summarizing the modern criticism and citing Empson prominently.

M57a Swan, Jim. "At Play in the Garden of Ambivalence: Andrew Marvell and the Green World." In *The Practice of Psychoanalytic Criticism*, ed. Leonard Tennenhouse. Detroit: Wayne State University Press, 1976. Pp. 189-201.

Reprint of M57.

M58 Tashiro, Tom. "Ambiguity as Aesthetic Principle." In *Dictionary of the History of Ideas: Studies of Selected Pivotal Ideas*, Vol. 1. Ed. Philip P. Wiener. New York: Scribner's, 1968. Pp. 48-60.

Broad survey of attitudes toward ambiguity in Western culture, with Empson mentioned as a central figure in the "semantic shift" away from ambiguity as a pejorative term to its modern equation with the "positive value of richness."

M59 Thwaite, Anthony. *Essays on Contemporary British Poetry*. Tokyo: Kenkyusha, 1957. Pp. 147-51.

M60 Tillyard, E.M.W. *The Muse Unchained: An Intimate Account of the Revolution in English Studies at Cambridge*. London: Bowes and Bowes, 1958.

An absorbing account of the subject of the subtitle, covering the years roughly from 1918 through 1935. The comment on *Seven Types* is notorious: "In 1930 Empson published his *Seven Types of Ambiguity*, a book which pushed the fierce and minute scrutiny of short texts very far and which showed that the new type of criticism had matured with surprising speed. Anyone quick to distinguish the rotten from the ripe and to sniff the taint of incipient corruption might now have guessed that an impulse had attained its maximum strength and that henceforward a decline or a coarsening must be expected." (P. 130.)

M61 Trevelyan, Julian. *Indigo Days*. London: MacGibbon and Kee, 1957.

Memoir by a Cambridge contemporary of Empson's, sketching that milieu and praising Empson as "by far the most brilliant member of the *Experiment* group." (P. 16.)

M62 Tuve, Rosemond. "On Herbert's 'Sacrifice.'" *Kenyon Review* 12 (1950), pp. 51-75.

Expanded in M62a. See annotation at M62a.

M62a Tuve, Rosemond. "'The Sacrifice' and Modern Criticism." *A Reading of George Herbert*. London: Faber and Faber; Chicago: University of Chicago Press, 1952. Pp. 19-99.

Expansion of M62. Takes exception to Empson's reading of Herbert's "The Sacrifice," claiming that the poet makes use of medieval liturgical and literary traditions: specifically, the Reproaches of Christ spoken from the Cross, and the Pleading of Christ tradition. Thus, the "effects" of the poem are not traceable solely to Herbert. The original discussion by Empson is in *Seven Types*, pp. 226-33. (See also D40, F78, and M27.)

M63 Wheelwright, Philip. "On the Semantics of Poetry." *Kenyon Review* 2 (1940), pp. 263-83.

Well known exposition of the "monosign" ("the atomic ingredient of literal language") and the "plurisign," which "tends to be" the "atomic ingredient of poetry" and the meaning of which is "partly contextual." Empson's ambiguity is "a looseness and duplicity of reference in would-be literal language," whereas plurisignation is "a controlled variation and plurality of reference in language that deliberately transcends the literal." Maintains that poetic statements differ from literal statements not in having subjective rather than objective references, "as Dr. Richards thinks," but in their "manner of asserting"--literal statements asserting "heavily," poetic statements with "varying degrees of lightness." These fundamental definitions appear in an argument that follows semantic complexity through three levels: atomic (the word), molecular (the statement), and organic (the "total statement"). (See M28.)

M63a Wheelwright, Philip. "On the Semantics of Poetry." In *Essays on the Language of Literature*, ed. Seymour Chatman and Samuel R. Levin. Boston: Houghton Mifflin Company, 1967. Pp. 250-63.

M64 White, Theodore, and Annalie Jacoby. *Thunder out of China*. New York: William Sloane Associates, 1946. Pp. 58-61.

Brief account of the movement of the Chinese universities inland during the years 1937-39 under pressure from Japanese invaders.

M65 *The Wykehamist*. Winchester School Magazine.

The Gardners say (H2, p. 35), "Empson's activities may be traced in issues of *The Wykehamist* from 27 February 1923 to 27 May 1925."

N

DISSERTATIONS

N1 Cole, David Anthony. "The Critical Writings of Mr. William Empson." Unpublished Doctoral Dissertation, Brandeis University, 1969. 285 pp.

A study of Empson's criticism that approves of his method of "releasing meanings through linguistic and psychological gambits," despite his tendency to "overread" literary texts.

N2 Johnson, Michael Lillard. "This Flickering of Wit: William Empson and the Psychology of Literary Forms." Unpublished Doctoral Dissertation, Rice University, 1968. 321 pp.

Studies chronologically both the poetry and the criticism of Empson from the point of view of Empson's psychology of language, finding the same assumptions behind both.

N3 Norris, Christopher C. "The Literary Criticism of William Empson." Doctoral Dissertation, University of London (University College), 1975.

Revised as *William Empson and the Philosophy of Literary Criticism*. (See annotation at H5.)

N4 Raeburn, Edward Cyril. "A Study of Verbal Analysis in the Critical Writings of William Empson." Unpublished M.A. Thesis, University of London, 1966.

N5 Wallace, Sarah Milstead. "Empsonian Pastoral and the Teaching of Undergraduates." Unpublished Doctoral Dissertation, George Peabody College for Teachers, 1976.

Takes from *Some Versions of Pastoral* the following concepts and studies their usefulness in teaching pastoral: putting the complex into the simple, the social values and criticism found in the pastoral, the double vision of pastoral, the fusion of heroic and pastoral traditions, ironical humility, comic primness, and the pastoral figure. Takes up these works as specimens of pastoral: *The Little Prince* by de Saint-Exupéry, *Howard's End* by E.M. Forster, and "The River" by Flannery O'Connor.

N6 Willis, John Howard, Jr. "The Poetry of William Empson." Unpublished Doctoral Dissertation, Columbia University, 1967.

Stresses Empson's debt to the Metaphysicals and discusses his relationship to Eliot and Yeats. Analyzes each of Empson's poems and finishes with an examination of his conceits, vocabulary, and other aspects of his style. Includes valuable appendices giving texts of uncollected poems and a list of commonly used words in his poetry.

AUTHOR INDEX

SUBJECT INDEX

INDEX OF PRIMARY TITLES

INDEX OF SECONDARY TITLES

WITHDRAWN
0_ / 13 / 2022
SAINT LOUIS UNIVERSITY